WoodSongs III

Front Porch Compendium
Social Commentary
Log Cabin Manual
and
SongFarmer's Notebook

by folksinger
Michael John

published by
POETMAN RECORDS USA
P.O. Box 200, Lexington, KY 40588

Music Transcriptions by
JOHN ROBERTS

BOOK and COMPACT DISC ISBN:
978-0-692-82754-3

Library of Congress Control:
2017930977

Special thanks to Loretta Sawyer, Bryan Klausing, Will Harvey, Lance Cowan,
Melissa Johnathon, Faith Quesneberry, Kevin Johnson, Rick Marks, my SongFarmer
friends and the WoodSongs Crew. Photos of Michael Johnathon by **Larry Neuzel**

A book by Michael Johnathon

WoodSongs III
Front Porch Compendium, Social Commentary,
Log Cabin Manual & SongFarmer's Notebook

An original collection of commentaries, short stories,
poetry, songs with music and tablature.

Table of Contents

C.F. Martin & Co.
EST. 1833

The Beginning ...

Gandhi said *"Where there is love, there is life."*

Love is a wonderful, amazing, powerful, and addictive need. It's the nuclear fuel that powers us when we have it ... and the crippling blow that stops us cold when taken away. Love is our most powerful joy hanging by a fine thread connected to our greatest pain.

"Abandonment is no less a betrayal than adultery;
no less cruel than abuse; no less painful than death ..."

Whewn lost it's like being adrift in a stormy black sea, losing sight of the shore. You can't breathe and you can't keep your head above the churning waters no matter how hard you try as you desperately strain to navigate yourself toward anything that resembles safe land.

And that land is the unattainable idea of *Love, Family* and *Home.* Arriving at dry harbor, tired and exhausted and unsure, you crawl toward a dream seeking an allusive paradise of affection and confidence that you are completely untrained and unprepared to recognize. Love becomes an crushing internal tsunami that you do not understand, yet desperately need.

You drag yourself upon the sandy shore with no maps, no navigation, no sense of direction. It's like walking through an island peppered with land mines, detonating and exploding around you. With each step you cup your ears in anticipation of the next thunderous roar of heartache. But you are used to it. You expect it. You have learned the fine art of *tolerating the intolerable* as you keep moving forward no matter what, hating every moment and yet unable to change it. And the relationships that you form seem to be with others walking the same path and navigating the same mine fields.

And when you finally find that delicate rose of love, that paradise of home and family, that precious yet unkind *'moment of deception'* where you actually give your whole self, heart and life force to it ... the storms of your youth come surging back as the mines explode at your feet. You are left alone in complete disbelief as you again pick up the smoldering, charred pieces of every dream you had.

And when the smoke finally clears and the thunder subsides, you step forward again ... cupping your ears and bracing, waiting, anticipating the next detonation, the next rumble from the storm.

To me, the Front Porch represents the shelter from that storm. To me, the front porch has three meanings: the *literal,* actual front porch on a home. The *emotional* front porch of finding the love of your life. And the *global, universal* front porch between nations. Those three viewpoints are bound up in that song.

This book is mostly about family, about love and the powerful keys that make it work: *Pride & Forgiveness.* Is a literary search for the emotional front porch we all desperately search for.

Gandhi said *"Where there is love, there is life."*
I used to believe that, but I'm not so sure anymore.

I have learned through time that so many function each day battered by rejection, exist without love as they search for emotional paradise. Most of us live within the prison of extreme heartbreak and disappointment. It's a double edged sword: usually the one growing up without love is the first to withdraw love from those closest to them.

The road to paradise is fraught with pot holes and barriers. Forgiveness is the bridge that carries us over every obstacle. Forgiveness is the fuel that powers love forever. It is the glue that holds our inner front porch together. Without forgiveness, love is weak and fragile, it crumbles and withers from the slightest heat.

Gandhi should have said,
"Where there is forgiveness ... love will last forever."

That is the only possible road map to the lovely, poetic, calm, and peaceful paradise that I want ... the inner front porch that we all ache for deeply, whether we acknowledge it or not.

Folksinger, SongFarmer & Tree Hugger
michael@woodsongs.com

Dedicated to the kids:
Makayla Rayne & Caleb Johnathon
MichaelB, Rachel Aubrey & Melody Larkin

**"There is no remedy for love
but to love more."**
Henry David Thoreau

**"There is nothing more truly
artistic than to love."**
Vincent Van Gogh

"Forgiveness is choosing to love."
Mahatma Gandhi

Welcome to WoodSongs III.

This is a book about Music.
This is a book about Art.
And this is about the glue that binds it all together:
Forgiveness, Pride and something called
Love.
mj

"**I see a cello in a tree.**"
the Artist said.

"**There's no cello in a tree.**"
the people sneered.

"But, I see a cello in a tree,"
he said, and the people laughed.

"I see a cello in a tree,"
he repeated as he chiseled the wood.

"I see a cello in a tree,"
as the crowds pointed and rediculed.

"I see a cello in a tree,"
and the people gasped at what they saw happening.

"Why ... look! There's a cello in a tree!"
they cried as the Artist left with his chisel.

The Artist's job is to see the cello in a tree.

The Log Cabin

How hard can it be?
Why "not knowing much" can be very helpful.

When I was in high school I had three main loves: Music, art and woodshop.

I suppose if you are reading this book, the music part is self explanatory. It has won over the other two, although together the trinity of music-art-wood remain very important, passionate elements in my life.

In the previous book, *WoodSongs II,* I explained how drawing became a fascination when I read a vintage World Book Encyclopedia section about Charles Schulz, the creator of *Peanuts.* I would sit for hours copying, tracing and drawing each of his panels ... I would even duplicate the squiggly, slightly nervous look of his lettering.

I vividly recall sitting in my bedroom late one night, my sketch pad blazing with ideas in front of me when the thought of creating my very own cartoon strip hit me.

"How hard can it be?" I thought.

All I needed was to come up with my own original cartoon characters, three panel story lines and be able to draw them consistently week after week.

Heck, piece of cake I thought.

So, I started drawing bugs.

9

Yes, bugs.

"If Bugs Ruled the World" was the name of my cartoon strip and my characters came to life with pen and ink and, before you knew it, I had half dozen cartoon strips done.

Now what? On my parents table was the day's mail including the free weekly newspaper for the Mid-Hudson Valley area. Picking it up I searched quickly for a cartoon strip ... nothing.

Perfect! says I.

A newspaper with no cartoon strip is a newspaper that needs a cartoon strip, and I just happen to have a cartoon strip.

I oozed blissful ignorance as I packed up my original cartoon boards and mailed them to the editor with my hand written note letting them know I was available. And then I waited.

A month went by and I figured bugs may not be ruling the world after all, especially in a newspaper in the Hudson Valley, so I moved on with my creative direction. Kids can be that way, passionate to a fault and then totally disinterested.

Anyway, about three months later a letter came in the mail from the editor of that paper and he accepted my cartoon strip. They didn't just accept it, they were going to publish the cartoon in every single newspaper they owned in New York and Connecticut.

"Holy cow! I'm like Charles Schulz!" I thought.

They even included a check prepaying for 15 weeks of cartoons in spite of the fact I never mentioned what I wanted for them. But hey, that check was for $150, more money than I had ever seen for myself up to that point.

It never occurred to me that $10 a week for a published cartoon strip in 17 newspapers was well below slave labor rates.

All the same, I was excited. And grateful. I never had a cartoon strip before, never had a job doing any kind of art, had no clue what I was doing and had no knowledge of the craft. Yet, I ended up with my own cartoon strip when I was just 16 years old, published in papers across the New York area where I grew up.

Ignorance is often the fuel of bravery.
Which brings me to the log cabin ...

"How vain it is to sit and write
when you have not stood up to live."
Henry David Thoreau

Growing up in a divided home made me long for the comfort and peace of "home." In my search for it, I failed miserably, which is not unusual. That seems to be very common with anyone who grew up in a fractured, alcoholic family. Don't take that wrong, my mother and stepfather were good people, my brother and sister did the best they could. But there were problems that seep into the spirit of any kid growing up like that, like a disease on a time clock, waiting to reveal itself.

I never succumbed to those habits. To be clear: *I've never been drunk, never smoked a cigarette, never even tried pot or any other drug in my whole life.* I couldn't even start having wine with dinner until my mid-twenties and even now have an automatic shut-off switch in my head: two drinks of anything and I am *done*.

Not having a peaceful home full of comfort and love, I would seek it in other things. I found folk music to be part of that search. Folk music gave me a history I didn't feel I had, it was a family of songs and musicians I yearned for.

So, I would sing about home. I would sing about love. I would sing about neighbors. I would watch others with a home and how they treated their house, their family, their kids.

I wanted what I didn't have. But love and home takes skills I also didn't have, skills I wasn't taught. And I would stumble and fall as I tried to learn those skills. I'm not proud of the fact that I've been married before, I wish in my heart-of-hearts I had the emotional tools to keep a home life together so that Melody, Rachel and MichaelB could grow up with the very prize that I myself would seek out constantly.

But I failed as I learned.

As time went on I realized I was living Thoreau's own words: I was singing and writing about love, home and earth but I was living in an apartment. I was singing about family, but I lost mine. I was singing and writing about community and front porches, but I didn't own one. It was time for me to live what I was singing about ... so I began a search for my very first home.

And so it was, on a warm spring Saturday afternoon, I decided to take a drive and search for that home. Not just any home, I wanted my childhood dream home ... I aimed to find a log cabin in the woods with a stream on the property.

I grew up along the Hudson River in New York and I was a neighbor of Pete Seeger. Once I realized who he was ... I didn't at first, we just thought he was a crazy old guy who claimed to be a musician. I came to admire his by-the-bootstraps way of life. He built his own log cabin overlooking his beloved Hudson, cut the trees himself and planted a big garden each year. I always thought that was an incredibly romantic way to live.

Could I find that in Lexington, Kentucky? It's a wonderful hometown but not exactly a place of woods and streams. Oh sure, there is a plethora of beautiful, scenic horse farms but these are multi-million dollar properties. It is what I would call *elegantly* rural.

I'm a banjo player on a folksinger's budget.

I needed to find low budget rural ... a *rustic, hard core, wood chopping, flannel shirt, tree hugger, fix-it-up-with-my-own-two-hands-rebuild-it-if-I-have-to* kind of rural.

How hard can that be? I wondered.

So, on this beautiful spring afternoon I set out to find my dream home. I asked around, collected the addresses of possible cabins from friends, real estate folks, Craigslisters and social media. Off I went, starting out early in the day. Cabin after cabin, I searched. And, lo and behold, every single log cabin for sale in this region was either sitting right on a main road or was priced beyond my ability to even think about. The cheapest log cabin I found was $600,000-plus on two crowded acres.

By the end of the day I was feeling less than hopeful. There was one more log home to see. Oddly enough, it was on the same road my little farm house rental was on.

I drove past a long, high, bending, winding rock fence and looked for the driveway right after it. The dirt drive came into view, and down the little lane I went, past hay fields toward a line of trees. The driveway turned downward and stright into ... a creek. A creek? I have to drive into a creek to get to this cabin?

Down into the creek I went, into the water and up the other side. And there is was, sitting on top of a hill, surrounded by pine trees ... a log cabin with a grand front porch. Waiting for me.

I was stunned. It was perfect.

I could mutter the only appropriate thing possible:

"Pete!" I yelled.

I found the Kentucky version of Pete Seeger's log cabin.

The log cabin, a photo taken the very day I found it

It's not like Pete Seeger was my big inspiration, it's just that he was only one of a couple people I knew who actually lived in one. He was my reference point.

I walked up the hill and the first thing I did was sit on the swing of the great front porch. I whipped out my cell phone and took a picture. The front cover of my *Front Porch* album is the shot I took that very day ... heck, I didn't even know who owned the ding-dang thing.

The next day, I tracked down the person who owned the cabin, got the phone number and left a voice mail. And waited. And waited. And waited.

Good grief, this was like the cartoon strip all over again.

A month later, the owner of the cabin finally returned my call. She wasn't avoiding me, but she really didn't want to sell it. See, this was the dream home she and her husband built with their own two hands. He passed away a few years ago and, well, she wanted to keep it in the family.

OK, it sounds reasonable. But she didn't understand: this was my hard core, wood chopping, flannel shirt, tree hugger, fix-it-up-with-my-own-two-hands-rebuild-it-if-I-have-to log cabin. She *has* to sell it.

I was bummed. And I couldn't find anything else in the region that even came close to this little log cabin. It was perfect ... to

"Once a decision is made,
the universe conspires to make it happen."
Ralph Waldo Emerson

me, anyway. It was a log cabin on a hill, with a stream and woods, that sat on almost seven acres of land. Beautiful, rich, fertile land.

And I never owned a home before.

How hard can it be? to change this nice lady's mind.

I waited a couple weeks and called her again, left a nice message. No response. Finally a few weeks later she returned my call.

"Honestly," she said. *"The cabin will probably be inherited by my daughter and it needs to stay in the family."*

Strike two.

I left town to perform some concerts, came home and took a late afternoon drive back to the cabin, just to look at it.

It was being rented at the time to a nice fellow, but who wasn't really maintaining it. Trash was piled up everywhere. The roof was a faded rusting blue metal. The logs had been painted gray, the property was overgrown and not landscaped. Inside old shag carpet was everywhere, it was dark with small rooms, many of them with sheet rock covering up the wooden walls.

It needed some attention. It needed some care.

It needed some love.

So, I wrote her a long letter and pretty much said it straight ... the log cabin was beautiful but it was not being maintained. It needed TLC. I would do that. I would work hard and restore it and make it worthy of what she and her late husband intended for it.

And I included my secret weapon in the letter:

Two tickets to see Steve Martin and the Steep Canyon Rangers at the Opera House for a concert I was producing.

Yes, I was bribing her.

A week later she called me up,

"OK, you persistent fellow, let's talk."

Rachel and MichaelB helping me rip up the old flooring and install the wide plank southern pine. When it was done it shined like glass ... beautiful!

16

To get the loan I had to build a bridge across the creek
so me and MichaelB built a bridge ... how hard can it be?

We met for coffee at a little cafe right up the road from the cabin. And she couldn't have been more delightful. And kind. And full of history and tales and stories about when she and her husband built their little log cabin. And maybe, just maybe, she would think about selling it. And we left it at that ... maybe.

Well, she came to the Steve Martin concert. A few days later I stopped by to visit her at her home, she showed me a violin that had been in her family for years, so I had it repaired and fixed up for her.

Yes, I continued bribing her.

Finally, I got the call I wanted,

"So we decided the log cabin would be too much for my daughter to handle, and we like you, so ... if you want it we will sell it."

Wow!!!! But for how much? Most log cabins in the region were priced well above anything I could afford. This cabin was sitting on nearly seven acres of prime farmland in central Kentucky.

We met at the little cafe again, chatted for an hour and I finally asked, *"How much?"*

She responded, *"What can you offer?"*

I gave her my best "I'm-a-broke-folksinger-but-I-promise-to-take-care-of-it offer.

She blinked, she thought. She pondered. And she said the one word every man dreams to hear from any woman:

Yes.

The words hung in the cafe for what seemed like a century. I grabbed a napkin off the table, wrote the price down and asked her to sign it as confirmation so I could go to a bank with it.

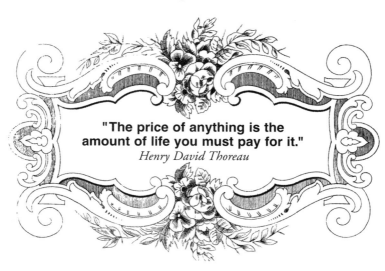

"The price of anything is the amount of life you must pay for it."
Henry David Thoreau

A freakin' *napkin*, people.

But she did it. She signed the napkin.

I left the cafe with gold in my hands ... a coffee stained napkin promising that the only log cabin in Kentucky that I could possibly afford could be mine.

The owner of the log cabin holds up our napkin agreement that helped me get the loan at the Windy Corner Cafe.

All I needed now was a bank loan.

I never had a bank loan before.

Heck, I never owned a home before.

"How hard can that be?" I wondered.

Well, pretty hard.

America was on the heels of the worst recession in modern history. Just a couple years earlier most credit cards stopped working for a week. The banking system nearly crashed, economies worldwide remained in turmoil. The jobless rate was skyrocketing. The housing market imploded and banks weren't lending.

And Mr. Folksinger wanted a home loan. Great timing.

I had my small deposit, having saved for this moment for several years. Because the cost of the cabin was low enough, my deposit would be high enough.

Because I rarely use a credit card and don't buy much, my credit rating was through the roof, over 800 points.

The way it works is you apply with your bank, they approve it and send it off to Fannie Mae for financing. So, I hit up my bank that I'd been with for years first. I figgered it should be a no brainer.

Actually, it was a no-loaner.

They sent it to Fannie Mae for approval, who sat on it for three weeks and turned me down. Off I go to a second bank. Application was good, deposit was good, credit rating is good ... four weeks later: Fannie Mae says no loan.

This went on for nearly six months.

All I had was a dream, a napkin and a very patient owner who, for some reason, decided she really wanted me to have her log cabin.

But, Fannie Mae told every bank no loan on the log cabin.

My last hope was a small lender that was technically not even a bank. A friend recommended that I try AgCredit because the log cabin has almost seven acres and they deal with mainly rural properties.

Off I go, knowing this was probably my last chance. Unlike the banks, these guys actually came out to visit the log cabin and walk the property. Impressive. We go through the drill: deposit good, credit good, application good, price good. Off it goes to Fannie Mae and for the seventh time, Fannie Mae says "no loan."

Well, the president of AgCredit, Jim Caldwell, got royally upset at this ... mind you, I never met Mr. Caldwell.

He calls me up,

"This is crazy, this is why people are marching in the streets. There is no good reason you should not be able to have a home. So, we decided to finance it for you in-house and forget Fannie Mae."

Unbelievable, I stumbled upon probably the only financial institution in America that would lend money to a folksinging banjo player who wanted to buy his first fixer-upper, a log cabin of all things.

And they did it.

Two months later we sat at a table and I signed a mountain of documents. Because the price was so reasonable they gave me a bit more than I needed to I could make upgrades. They cut a check and handed it to the former owner and I walked out of AgCredit so deep in debt I couldn't see straight.

But *very* happy.

I drove to the cabin late that afternoon, stared at the colossal job in front of me to repair, upgrade, fix, maintain and nurture a log cabin. Then it hit me:

"Dude, you're not a carpenter ... you're a banjo player."

This would be a project for experienced construction workers with tools I didn't have, knowledge I didn't have and wisdom I didn't have. I needed to get all three and quick.

"How hard can it be?" I wondered.

Pretty ding-dang hard.

But thanks to YouTube and *This Old House* on PBS I learned what I needed to learn. The first thing I did was get a chain saw and take down the log wall separating the kitchen from the dining room and opened up the space between the small rooms. I ripped out the shag rugs, pulled hundreds of nails out of the floor joists and put in new southern pine plank flooring. I pulled down the sheetrock and then hand rubbed tongue oil into the walls to bring out their luster. I built porches outside the kitchen, and big 20' x 24' back deck and ... thinking the house was *"one room short of a wife"* ... put in a 20x20' log addition. This was my music room and then became the twins bedroom in short order. I'll explain that part later.

Because I was on a tight budget, I had to do everything myself in between concerts, songwriting, WoodSongs and more. It was insane but I loved it ... including building a bridge over the creek, something AgCredit required to be done within one calender year. I got it done, just me and MichaelB, in only seven months. I decided that my "payment" for all the work would be to own the tools it took to do the job, so now I have a mighty fine work shop that used to be a horse stall in the back meadow.

By the way, the local *Habitat ReStore* is a great place to find amazing deals. I built this writer's cabin in the back field ... my studio get-away and now man-cave ... for a whopping $1,700 using almost all repurposed materials from the *ReStore*.

So why am I telling you the story of the cartoon strip and the log cabin? I have a reason, it's called Love. You'll hear it a lot as we go through this book together.

A by-product if love is pride. When you have pride in what you love, it motivates you to take care of it, to nourish it, to work hard on its behalf and maintain it. Pride in what you love also fuels the power you need to dive into unknown, uncharted waters.

Whether it's a cartoon strip, a book, a log cabin, the dinner dishes, the laundry or an international radio and TV broadcast, love and pride supercedes experience, and makes whether or not you've done something before irrelevant.

The words of Thoreau come to mind. He was certainly a hard worker and thought long and deep about what he was doing and why. He always searched to find the value in all of his endeavors.

And lawd, lawd that man loved his woodpile.

"Every man looks with pride
upon his woodpile ..."
Henry David Thoreau

Face it, chopping wood by hand is not easy. It's work. It could easily be something to hate and dread, but Thoreau did not view it that way. He had pride. He found joy in his work.

Pride takes the drudgery out of work.

Pride adds excitement to work as you anticipate its finish.

Pride is the reward you feel after doing good work.

Pride makes you fix things without complaining.

Pride makes work worth it.

The rustic log cabin dining room, ready for company and conversation. On the right side you can see where I took down the log wall to open it up into the kitchen

This is the inside of the Writer's Cabin - built after I finished work on the log cabin home. It served as my studio during the SongFarmer iPhone Album recordings

I don't mind the work it takes to maintain a home, or launch a project, make a bed, to introduce a song, or even live past the harsh words of a critic .... because pride in my home, my song, my project is an element of the fuel that makes it all happen.

Pride keeps the bed made, the grass mowed, the office clean, the car orderly, the guitar in tune and the song performed well. Pride makes you show up on time. Pride makes you prepared. Pride makes you keep your word. Pride is Free. And powerful. Pride and Love, when fused together involves your entire being, your whole heart.

Our log cabin home as it looks today, sitting rustic and lovely on top of a hill overlooking a stream and woods.

It costs *nothing* to keep your yard clean, your house in order and litter out of the creek. Hometowns with pride are excited to have clean-up days, schools find willing students to keep their classrooms in order. Pride makes you do it *right* when you do it. Half-assed, partially-done, and sloppy isn't "right."

I think our welfare culture has stripped many good, working people of their pride, and that is one of the things tilting our communities off-balance.

"I lost my heart to the whole idea ..."

Pete Seeger explaining the fire behind his dream of building the Clearwater. Pride is the fuel of every good thing we do, whether raising a family or raising the sails of a boat to clean a river. And if we struggle and fail, take a deep breath and try again.

Jack was going to be married, so his dad sat him down for a little father-son chat.

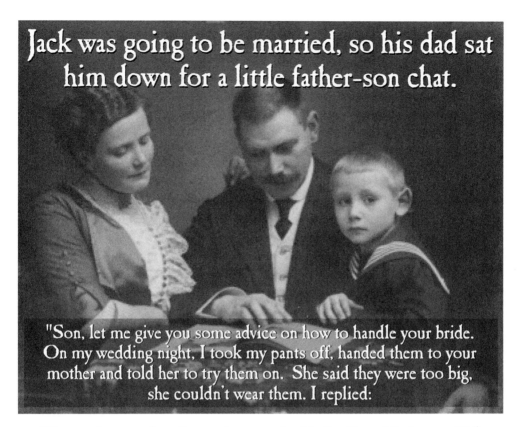

"Son, let me give you some advice on how to handle your bride. On my wedding night, I took my pants off, handed them to your mother and told her to try them on. She said they were too big, she couldn't wear them. I replied:

"Remember, my dear, I wear the pants in this family and I always will."

Well, young Jack thinks he might try this on his honeymoon, so the night comes and he takes his pants off and says,

"Here babe, try these on." She does and found they didn't fit.

"Exactly," he says. "I wear the pants in this family and don't you to ever forget that."

His new wife pauses, then takes off her little pants, "Here, try mine on."

Jack says, "You know I can't get into your pants."

She pats his hand and says, "Exactly ... and if you don't change your attitude you never will."

"Let the wife make the husband glad to come home, let the husband make her sorry he leaves."
Martin Luther

"We need a Front Porch 'round the World ..."

Melissa sings on the grand front porch of our log cabin

The Lost Power of America's
Front Porch

It's a melodic early morning on the front porch of my log cabin here in Kentucky. The air gently resonates with a magical, peaceful symphony of sounds ... sunrise is nature's orchestral awakening, an earth-song that starts the day.

Henry David Thoreau, my favorite writer, said it best,

"The morning is the awakening hour. All poets emit their music at sunrise. To him whose elastic and vigorous thought keeps pace with the sun ... the day is a perpetual morning."

And so, in this calm and tranquil setting, I sit in a rocking chair with my cup of cinnamon coffee and begin scribbling thoughts in this old ledger. The irony of writing about this is subject not lost on me. There is a connection, a spiritual and emotional thread, that connects family, community, love, music and earth together ... and it is well represented by a front porch.

How so?

Once upon a time, America loved itself.

It loved what it was, what it stood for, what it was going to be. Isn't that the journey of every origanized people, community and civilization throughout history? They begin with tremendous promise and fiery passion ... then relax and settle into the reflection of their illusions only to quickly lose the heart and spirit of what they aspired to be. Even today, we look around us and realize we are but a pale shadow of the moral greatness we hoped for.

As Gandhi watched his beloved India ripping itself apart he said: *"Where there is love, there is life."*

Gandhi's point is that love is the very glue that holds this fragile human life together on this planet.

I observe our hometowns, our communities and the world and wonder, *"What is so different today? What has changed from just a few decades ago, when we were riding high on the vision of everything we thought we could be?"*

It occurred to me that, among other things, we have lost our sense of home, our sense of belonging, our sense of community. We are the most transient and unstable generation in America's history. We have surrendered our connection to nature and replaced it with air conditioned work cubicles and two dimensional online friends. We limit our communication with each other to 140 character tweets. We live in apartments and neighborhoods without ever meeting or caring to know our neighbors.

The point is we no longer live in organic communities. Most people don't "love" where they are, therefore they don't have much incentive to make it better. We lost our sense of the "front porch." Heck, most new homes don't even have front porches. They were abandoned with the advent of air conditioning and television as people retreated indoors and away from each other.

The front porch was once the center stage of a family's community spirit, where neighbors gathered for music, fellowship, coffee in the morning, ice tea in the afternoon, and watching the moon settle over the trees in autumn. It's where a young man would court the girl of his dreams while her family stood vigil inside the home.

The front porch was the grand pulpit of the neighborhood.

It's hard to love a home or community that we aren't actually part of. People don't have homes anymore ... houses have become temporary boxes in which to exist before moving on.

I believe, especially since 9/11, many people around the world are searching again for a sense of roots, family, and home. This is the army of treehuggers, folksingers and SongFarmers. It's the folks who bake their own bread, chop their own wood, cook Sunday dinners and pick up litter along the roadways. It's the hometown musicians with no place to play so they sing for free at local schools. It's fathers who take their sons camping instead of watching TV, moms who take their daughters to volunteer at a children's hospital instead of the mall.

They are looking for a sense of community that goes beyond the shallow, flat-screened world of the internet. They seek the genuine comfort of a hot cup of coffee at the breakfast table with family, the glass of wine in front of a winter fireplace with a loved one, the crunchy poetry of the autumn woods with their children.

This is the grand, global, emotional front porch that Gandhi alluded to. We are all looking to find our front porch, even if we live in trailer parks or third floor condos in a city.

To me, the Front Porch has three meanings and we will be exploring them in future pages together:

1) the *literal*, actual front porch on a home
2) the *emotional* front porch of finding the love of your life.
3) the *global*, symbolic front porch between nations.

Those three viewpoints are bound up in the title song of the "Front Porch" album. This book is a literary look at the emotional front porch we all search for and will give me a chance to explore and discuss matters that I find personally enriching and important.

To be clear: our love of home, community and music is an emotional roadmap that leads to the lovely, poetic, calm, and peaceful paradise that we seek ... the inner front porch that we all ache for deeply, whether we acknowledge it or not.

Gandhi said, *"Where there is love, there is life."*
He could have added:
"Where there is a front porch, there is community."

Our love of home can even defeat the greatest threat and bombastic, amoral, powerful enemy of our mother Earth: **money.**

I've been developing this idea since I was a kid. I was the one who would plant and then harvest the big family garden. My uncle even subscribed to *Mother Earth News* as a gardening gift for me. It was through those pages the concept of how to merge the earth, nature, community and home with music began to form, albeit in the most clumsy way possible.

As a young teenager I was introduced to the partnership of folk music and community through the example of my neighbor. He was a pleasant fellow, an odd older guy who claimed to be a musician ... but played the banjo. That was an oddity. After all, real musicians wouldn't be caught dead playing a banjo. To a young rocker like me if it doesn't plug in it's not a real instrument, right? Plus the guy was kinda weird. Anytime there was a big storm he would show up at our school yard with an ax so he could chop up any fallen trees and branches.

That was creepy. To us, anyway.

The week I graduated high school my buddy calls me up late one night with a fun idea.

"Dude, you wanna come work at a radio station?"
"How hard can it be?" says I.

So I pile everything I own into an old Toyota with 300,000 miles on it and drive 44 hours straight from upstate New York to Laredo, Texas to start my part-time minimum-wage job at KLAR-AM. You can do that when you're 18 because you're immortal. The reason I drove without stopping is because the car was an automatic but had a bad starter and, well ... you get the idea.

A few months later, about three in the morning, I had to pull an oldies song from the selection file and happened by chance to choose a record by Roger McGuinn and The Byrds called *"Turn, Turn, Turn."* As the song played over the air I noticed on the information card the tune was written by my crazy neighbor.

"Oh ... so that's who Pete Seeger is."

**Pete Seeger expounding
one of his many stories**

Yes, until that serendipitous moment I had no idea I was living next to folk music royalty, the legend who gave us *Where Have All The Flowers Gone, Turn, Turn, Turn, If I Had A Hammer,* and more. Pete was best friends with Woody Guthrie and Paul Robeson.

Dylan sings on a front porch

He introduced great songs to the world like *This Land Is Your Land* and *We Shall Overcome.* He introduced Bob Dylan and Joan Baez to the global front porch, and helped them find their audiences.

Realizing who Pete was became a musical ah-ha moment for me. By the time that three-minute record ended I decided I wanted to be a folksinger. I soon left Laredo and moved to a small Appalachian hamlet called Mousie, Kentucky and began traveling up and down the hollers with my guitar and banjo, learning songs and having scores of front-porch hootenannies with my neighbors.

Within weeks of beginning my romantic musical adventure, *Mother Earth News* entered the picture again. A neighbor had a stack

Front Porch

Words & Music
©Michael Johnathon/RachelAubreyMusic/BMI
Performed in the key of D (drop D tuning)

There's a front porch 'round the old home-place,

All my trou-bles dis-ap-pear with-out a trace.

And chil-dren play all sum-mer long.

The world feels right, and noth-ing's wrong. And fire-flies

dance on a star-ry night, 'Round the old front porch to-

night, 'Round the old front porch to-night.

There's a Front Porch 'round the old homeplace
where troubles disappear without a trace
 and children play all summer long
 the world feel's right like there's nothing wrong
 and fireflies dance on a starry night
 'round the old front porch tonight
 'round the old frontporch tonight

There's a Front Porch 'round my true loves eyes
I can sit and watch that girl all my life
 and in her eyes this world seems right
 she's a gentle and peaceful sight
 and since the day that girl became my wife
 I've had a Front porch 'round my life
 a Front porch 'round my life

We need a Front Porch 'round the world
We need a Front Porch 'round America
 Let's slow it down and learn to set a spell
 start serving lemonade instead of hell
 I wish these leaders could outlaw fear
 I wish they'd lead from a rockin' chair

We need a Front Porch 'round the world
A Front porch 'round the world
We need a Front Porch 'round the world

of back issues of the magazine and, after hearing me whine about the lack of entertainment opportunities appropriate for a young musician newly planted in the hollers of the mountains like myself, they thought some proper reading material might be helpful. I came home one day to find a stack of *Mothers* waiting for me on my porch steps.

Reading the magazines was fun and I was fascinated by articles about growing strawberries in an old rain barrel, French intensive gardening, bootstrap business ideas and raising chickens.

And then ... there it was.

Somewhere in the middle of the pile I pull out a 1982 back issue and it had *him* inside. Pete Seeger, my banjo-picking, ax-wielding neighbor was the feature story and *"Plowboy Interview"* of the month. I read about his environmental ideas, the Clearwater project and folk music. The whole ambient vision of how music, community and nature connected was like a white-hot lightning bolt through my head.

I closed the pages and felt my blood boil with energy. I decided to create a project I called *Earth Concerts,* a concert tour about nature, home and songs that encouraged the audience to pick up litter and take care of their communities that I would perform to schools all across the nation.

Wait a minute ... I never did a concert tour before.

"How hard can it be?" I wondered.

Pretty hard ... but it worked, and over the course of the next few years I performed nearly 2,500 Earth Concerts attended by 3

million people in colleges, high schools, county fairs and libraries in 14 states across America. I was on a journey to use music for something better than selling records, to play songs for reasons greater than becoming a star.

And now it seems I have come full circle. Here I am on this quiet Kentucky morning, writing on the front porch of my log cabin about organic music, nature and community.

I hope I can encourage you to think about the wonderful, passionate world of acoustic songs, homemade music, coffeehouse concerts and neighbors singing together. I want to share ideas and experiences that will encourage you to use your music in special and effective ways so they become real in your musical world, your front porches and living rooms, your neighborhoods and your home towns.

Together we will take the spotlight away from concert halls and arenas and focus instead on the most brilliant, important and beautiful stage in the world:

Your own front porch.

SongFarmer: Any artist, poet, painter or musician that uses their art to make their homes, lives, and communities better.

SongFarmer.

It's a great word.

Much better than "folksinger" or songwriter or performer. It is a poetic way to describe someone who uses their music to plant artistic seeds in their communities, families and their careers.

Here's a fact: the music business has really changed the past few years. Actually it's been turned upside down and artists have been rocked to the core. They need help and encouragement. They need a new direction because the old way of doing things no longer works.

They need honesty. I noticed a couple years ago that Folk Alliance, IBMA and the Americana Association all had one thing in common: they were well intentioned albeit expensive-to-attend trade organizations in a music world of collapsing trade. They are music business trade groups that try to help musicians, record labels and agents connect to enhance the artist's careers ... but mostly ineffective, I found, when it came to actually helping artists.

Why? Because reality often supercedes good intentions. Music stores are gone, cars are being made with no CD players, booking agents aren't signing because venues are shutting down, record labels aren't signing because nobody is buying CDs anymore. Meanwhile, these trade groups collect membership fees from artists to attend conventions based on business models that no longer exist. It is almost funny if it wasn't so sad ... their conventions are filled with artists who wrangle to get a showcase just to end up performing in front of other frustrated artists who wished they had your time slot. A futile, expensive endeavor that accomplishes little, if anything.

In my travels around the country, and I'm sure you see the same, the community of artists are adrift with no direction as the norms of our "market place" evaporate and collapse around us. These trade groups are run by very sincere people but are beholden to obsolete, outdated business models that are no longer valid or useful. Frankly, BMI and ASCAP have the same issues.

What is left, what is real, what is truthful are the tens of thousands of front porch minded musicians who love music, who love to play, who love to sing, who love to write ... but who will never make a living at it. They are worthy of validation without being lured to become members of an expensive trade group.

"We need something new, something more better-er," says I.

Creating the WFPA

To help artists deal with the changes in the music world, I wanted to organize a grand international association of front-porch minded musicians.

"How hard can it be?" I wondered.

Pretty ding-dang hard.

With the help of some talented, caring, and experienced friends of mine we organized the *WoodSongs Front Porch Association (WFPA)* ... an alternative to other great efforts like the Folk Alliance, the IBMA or the Americana Music Association. The WFPA doesn't compete in any way with those very fine folks.

The truth is there is no music "business" anymore. Not for the tens of thousands of artists playing at farmers markets, retirement homes, small noisy clubs, schools and front porches across the land.

I am describing the world of artists who are gathering on front porches and living rooms, turning the TV off and inviting friends over to sing and play in exchange for a pot luck meal and some homemade cookies. These are the true *Troubadours of America,* those who will sing in a local school to show kids what a banjo is, who play in a burn ward at a children's hospital or who comfort the retired with a few songs at an old folks home.

They play for the pure love of music and willingly sing where "lack of money" stop others from going.

These are the untrained and inexperienced, planting seeds with their music and nourishing a global garden with their songs. They are the tired and the exhausted from years of trying. The passionate and hungry who want to make a difference. The brilliant but unknown. The rejected and declined.

They are the front porch community of musicians and artists the marketplace crushed with non-response.

These talented, sincere songwriters, performers, dreamers and artists are being asked to pay for association fees, conference fees, travel, hotels and meals ... often totalling $1000 or more. Instead of being helped to understand what to do with a garage full of unsold CDs in a world with no more record stores, you might be treated to a two hour speech that has nothing to do with music or the issues at hand.

Surely we can do more better-er.

We call the members of the WFPA "SongFarmers"

Enter the *WoodSongs Front Porch Association*
We call our members *SongFarmers.*

A SongFarmer is any artist, songwriter, musician, poet and dreamer who uses their art and music to make their lives, homes and communities better.

To a SongFarmer, the front porch is as important a stage as a concert hall. Their banjo is a community plow, their songs are like seeds, their guitar is a hammer and saw. Music is an issue of the heart, not their wallet. They don't make fans, they make friends.

My argument for the SongFarmer movement is that it is time to create a community based on honesty. The fact is most of these wonderful songwriters and artists will never be able to make a living playing music. There is no shame in that. The crime comes when they are charged more to attend a conference supporting a non-existant market than most of them will earn in a year.

So the question is, if we create a community of like minded artists, what do we do with all of that energy?

Aside from a massive roots music education program that goes free to teachers and home school families (SongFarmers.org/classroom) we engaged the home communities by starting SongFarmers Chapters, now in scores of cities including the latest as I write this in the Virgin Islands. We expect to have well over 200 involved in the next two years, and we need one in *Your Hometown,* too. Our members gather their friends and neighbors to sing, share pot luck and create friendships in

music. The SongFarmers Chapter in little Tellico Plains TN averages 50-60 attending each event. They visit retirement homes, schools, hometown gazebos and downtown parades.

They sing, they write, they play, they stay busy. This is much better, and healthier, than sitting home counting rejection letters from record labels about to go out of business.

And, lo and behold, our SongFarmers create an audience that didn't exist before. They work for Free. They work for Love. They work for the audience ... and the audience does what the audience always does: buy their stuff.

The WoodSongs broadcast helped pioneer that business model and was created in the belief that love is the greatest transaction of the arts. It is the only transaction that matters. It causes hearts, minds and wallets to open. The music business is failing because they focused on money and not what causes the money: Love.

Here's an example I use often: no one in the history of music ever bought an album because it said "RCA Records." They bought it because they *loved* Elvis. End of story. They could care less about the record company. They would have bought his albums if he was selling them out of his 1953 Buick station wagon.

Love sells everything in the arts. WoodSongs has created a weekly audience of well over 2 million people on 514 radio stations plus American Forces Radio in 173 nations and 96M USA TV homes on PBS because of the love transaction.

Love creates incredible, powerful things and its greatest accomplishment is that it can create a massive audience. On WoodSongs yours truly works for free, the engineers and TV directors work for free, the 36 member crew are all volunteers, the theatre is donated, local hotels put the artists up for free, local restaurants feed them and the crew for free. The show goes free to public radio, free to the American Forces Radio Network, free to public television. Even the artists who come on the show are volunteers and don't even get a travel stipend.

And now you know why folk rhymes with broke.
Just kidding ... sorta :)

Yet Judy Collins has been on WoodSongs six times, Tommy Emmanuel nine times, Bela Fleck five times. Why? Because "free" built a massive audience and the audience does what the audience ALWAYS does ... buy the artist's stuff. And artists sell stuff when they come on WoodSongs, so the fact they do it for free becomes irrelevant.

The FREE business model

Free is the new business model of the Arts.
Before you gag, let me explain.

"Free" has always been a viable business model. For decades record companies send the album to radio for free, the station plays it for free, the audience listens on their favorite station for free. And if they end up LOVING the artist, they run to a record store and buy the album, and concert ticket, and t-shirt ... Free is the fastest way to generate an *audience,* who are in fact the greatest benefactors of the arts.

Don't believe me?

Facebook created a multi-billion dollar empire by letting users have the platform FREE. Google, iTunes, YouTube ... all free and they are all worth billions. Why? Because FREE generates an audience, and once anything has an audience, wallets will open. FREE as a business model is viable. What the music business and most artists forgot was the LOVE part. I know it sounds very kumbaya and all, but it's true.

So my point is this:
Free works. Just don't be afraid to use it.

The more good work an artist does for the love of it, even if free, the bigger their audience will get. The bigger the audience, the better odds of them making a living. So, in a very real sense, focusing on money instead of the audience, focusing on trade instead of the heart, FA and IBMA are actually interfereing with artist's ability to make a living.

I believe any financial transaction that prevents an artist from reaching their audience is a bad deal, which is why BMI and ASCAP need to change their business model. They have to get the heck out of the way of artists reaching the audience and stop making it cumbersome for venues to present live music. It's a dinosaur of a system and it has got to be upgraded. I expound on this later.

Which brings me back to the world of SongFarmers.

The community of front-porch minded musicians make up the actual audience of roots music. That audience is special, it's talented and worthy of cultivation. Ever notice where the best music gets played at a folk or bluegrass festival? It's not on the main stage ... it's in the parking lots and campgrounds. Folk music, for all it's genres, is best played by members of its own audience. Usually for free.

The WFPA and our SongFarmer members are simply organizing that audience and giving them a positive direction for their talents, heart and music. We do this honestly. Let's stop pretending a market exists for them where there is none.

This community of "musical deplorables" has tremendous power and potential, and by tapping into it you can accomplish great, wonderful, unheard of things. And accomplishing good things, in the end, is the best PR campaign for any artist.

I'll use Pete Seeger as an example. Yes, again. Sure he was a good songwriter and fine banjo picker and he had his fan base, albeit damaged by the communist hunt. But his greatest, global PR campaign was something he did for free: *The Clearwater.* It gained him genuine, complete respect, it made him an inspiration to tens of thousands of musicians and millions of people.

It took work, effort, thought, planning and gumption far beyond sitting in his log cabin decrying his banishment from TV and loss of a record deal. He fought back by accomplishing something good ... even it was for free. And he did it as a local citizen in his local community. It was all hometown stuff.

The result was this new legion of admirers worldwide that bought his concert tickets and his albums. And he earned the very thing you notice most folk musicians don't have:

Respect.

Harry Chapin did the same. Benefit after benefit, helping where he could, giving of his heart, music and mind. People weren't just his fans, they were his friends. He made his hometown just as important as any national stage. He learned that from Pete Seeger. Pete and Harry humbly treated their audience as if they were "unfamous."

**Pete planted the seeds ...
SongFarmers cultivate
the Garden**

The byproduct of humility is often praise. It galvanized his audience, and his career was bolstered by the one thing most one-hit-wonders can only dream of:

Respect.

Respect is not awarded by virtue of our vocation. It is earned.

The reason, since antiquity, most musicians are not recognized as working people is because, frankly, most of them don't do or accomplish much. The cliche' has become real, especially as the market collapses. If I meet another whiner sitting around their basement with a small recording machine waiting to be discovered I'll scream. Get off your duff and show the world you actually want this. WORK for heaven's sake and stop complaining. The point the WFPA makes to our SongFarmers is this:

Artists should not just think outside the box, they need to *crush the box* and build a new one.

And the new box for musicians is local, not national. The "new box" means they probably won't make a living with their music, but it can be a powerful and effective part of their life.

Every national career is launched from our "front porch" and my goal is to make that stage important again and help pave a way for artists to be less discouraged by what is happening to this music business.

With the WFPA I wanted a new way to reach out to artists, to really explain the new music world, and really point to a brand new direction for their music and careers. I wanted this to be really, really, really cheap, just $25 a year. And to attend our yearly conference, called The *WoodSongs Gathering*, they get to come free ... yes, as in free.

And before all you finger-waggers get started, I'm not putting down the trade groups. Heck, I'm even a member. I do, however, think they are lost in an old business model that no longer exists. The music world is upside down and inside out. Who would have guessed just five years ago that today one of the biggest retailers of CDs in America would end up being a restaurant chain? And, no, it's not Starbucks.

We all need to have a brand new outlook on music. We need to have a truthful, albeit painful look at what is really happening out there. We need a spectacular new direction for our music. And we all have to learn, as brutal as it may seem at first, how FREE works.

SongFarmers are taught the most important rule of the new music world: LOVE is the most important transaction of the arts. It isn't marketing, management, what record label you're on or who your investor is. All of that is irrelevant without LOVE. "Love" makes the world of art work.

Nashville has virtually lost it's entire music middle class because the bean counters focused on marketing and money ... not love. The only thing ... the only thing ... the audience responds to is their love for a song, love for an artist, love for an idea.

SongFarmers learn to direct that love in a way that does not focus on money. They focus instead on their families, their hometowns, their audiences and resurrect the emotional front porch in everyone who hears them.

Where the SongFarmer name came from

This all started when I performed a concert in Winnsboro, Texas and two songwriter friends, Lynn Adler and Lindy Hearne, gave me a bumper sticker that proclaimed their pondside cabin home in Texas an "organic song farm." It sat on my desk for months and then one day, as I was organizing the *WoodSongs Front Porch Association* it occurred to me that "song farming" is exactly what we are trying to do.

Our members would be called *SongFarmers*.

I called them up and said would you mind if we stole your word? They said, go ahead, we stole it from someone else.

It was so Woody Guthrie-ish ...

"Aw he just stole from me. But I steal from everybody. Why, I'm the biggest song stealer there ever was."
Woody Guthrie

And that's where the SongFarmer name came from. I think Woody was a SongFarmer. So was Jean Ritchie and Pete Seeger. So is most of the music world filled with artists who love playing more than most anything else.

So join the WFPA. Become a SongFarmer. Change your thinking about the music business for the better, and be part of the amazing work our members are doing. **SongFarmers.org**

The WFPA mission statement:

To gather the global community of front porch minded musicians, bring roots music education into schools free of charge, and enhance communities by redirecting the energies of local musicians.

The Significance of the FEATHER

I'm asked often about two things: the *medal* on my jacket and the *feather* on my guitar. Let's talk about the feather.

A few years ago a friend of mine was explaining his Native American history and how they believed dreams were like living creatures carried on the wings of eagles.

"How beautiful," says I. So I went and found myself an Indian dreamcatcher with a feather on it, tied it to my guitar thinking, *"Songs are like dreams, carried on the wings of voices."*

Sometime later, I was told a dreamcatcher is actually a sacred thing to many Native Americans, who are offended by having them sold as cheap trinkets in tourist shoppes.

"What about just a feather?" says I.
No problem.

So I found some hawk feathers, fashioned them to hook on my tuning gears and I've been letting them hang from my guitar and banjo ever since. In my vision the feather signifies the spirit and heart of song, carried by the voices of the audience is if by an eagle, soaring high over us and beyond.

And, to me, that's what a good song should do …

Pick it, Play it, Perform it ...

SongFarmers BLUES

Words & Music
©Michael Johnathon/RachelAubreyMusic/BMI
Performed in the key of G

This is a fun song and should be played with a loose, relaxed "front porch" feel. Listen to the recording, but certainly come up with your own style. You might even add a verse, especially if you want to add a different "instrument" to the lyric mix.

VERSE

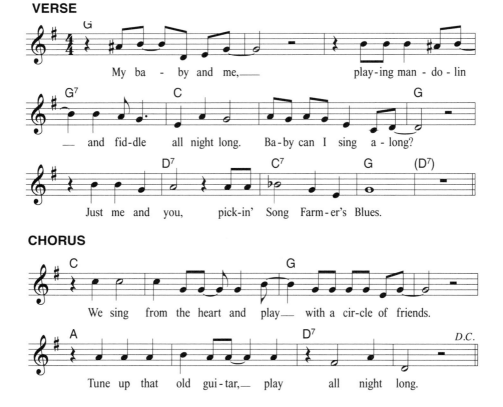

My ba - by and me,___ play-ing man - do - lin ___ and fid-dle all night long. Ba-by can I sing a - long? Just me and you, pick-in' Song Farm-er's Blues.

CHORUS

We sing from the heart and play___ with a cir-cle of friends. Tune up that old gui-tar,___ play all night long.

My Baby and Me
    Playin' mandolin and fiddle
    All night long
        Maby I can sing along
        Just me and you ... pickin' SongFarmers Blues

On a Front Porch Swing
    Pickin' to the rhythm
    And a neighbor calls
        "Maybe I can play with you"
        It don't have to be new ... playin' SongFarmers Blues

        We sing from the heart
        And play with a circle of friends
            Tune up that old guitar
            and play All Night Long ...

My banjo and me
    I can play any song and make it
    sound so sweet
        like a 5-string symphony
        but so can you ... playin' SongFarmers Blues

(inst)

        We sing from the heart
        And play with a circle of friends
            Tune up your old guitar
            and play All Night Long ...

This Martin and Me
    Your mandolin and fiddle
    all night long
        No one has to play alone
        Just me and you ... playin' SongFarmers Blues
        Me and you ... playin' SongFarmers Blues

Let's Discuss the
PIG

An overview of the main problem with most Careers, Bands, Music & Arts organizations.

Once upon a time there was a farmer ...

... and he had a wonderful, vibrant garden that fed his family, his livestock, even his neighbors. It was so healthy and food so plentiful he had enough produce for his local market. Yes, his garden even provided him with an income.

The farmer loved his garden, he was proud of it, he tended it, took care of it, cultivated it, watered it and gave it all of his attention.

Then, one day, the farmer got himself a pig.

And, oh my, how impressed he was with his pig, so new and different from the garden. The farmer became so enamored with the pig that he began to give it more of his time. His pig grew and got fat and the farmer fed it more and more of the garden's produce.

Soon, most of the harvest from his garden was gathered just to feed the pig. The pig demanded so much attention the farmer had less time to tend his garden ... and so the harvest began to whither and dry up. Weeds began to take over the garden but the farmer hardly noticed because his attention was so consumed by his pig.

One day the farmer was so exhausted from caring for the pig that he asked himself, *"How did this pig get so fat, and what happened to my beautiful garden?"*

But still the pig demanded more from the garden, more time and attention from the farmer. And the farmer couldn't escape the demands of the pig. He began to lose his joy with the pig, with the garden and all the good things he once had as a loving farmer.

Until finally, one day, there was nothing left of the garden.
It was gone ... and the pig couldn't survive and the farmer had nothing for market and couldn't feed his family.

What is THE PIG?

Let's use music to explain, but this is true of all artists, bands, charities and non-profits. In my universe of folk and roots music, our "garden" is the world of songs, poetry, community, instruments, the audience and all that is part of being a musician and songwriter. It is a beautiful, amazing, colorful, vibrant garden.

And there are many loving, attentive "farmers" for this world: the IBMA takes care of the bluegrass garden, the Folk Alliance cares for the folk garden, etc.

The "pig" is the corporate structure of any organization ... whether a national charity, a local community group or a garage band. It is the business entity created to oversee their operations. The "pig" is how expensive you make your existance.

Here's what happens:

When the pig is first brought into the garden, the expenses are low and all the attention is on the music, the artists and the garden itself. The good intention is to make the garden bigger and better while feeding the pig.

Remember, the garden existed long before the pig, but once the pigs arrive they tend to take over the garden. As the pig grows the need for money takes over ... for Executive Director salaries, offices, managers, staff, marketing, vacations and benefits. Travel budgets. All of this money gets sucked out of the garden. The bigger the pig gets the more unyielding the budgets become and the more attention the farmer gives the pig instead of tending the garden.

Before you know it the garden begins to whither and dry up. The cost of being members of the organization get way too high. The cost of attending the conferences get way too high. The pig overtakes the garden to such a degree that all the beauty that was the garden begins to dry up and leave. Feeding the pig makes the cost of being in the garden too expensive for the average artist.

It costs the average musician upwards of $1000 to be a member of most music trade groups, pay for conference fees, travel and get hotel rooms and meals. That is more than most musicians make in a year.

If it costs more to be part of the garden than the garden can provide, the farmer needs to make a choice:

Abandon the garden - or get rid of the pig.

My whole argument here is that the corporate structure of the arts world ... the pig ... has gotten so out of hand that it is ruining the very garden of arts we love. As the business models change and the ability of artists to make a living becomes more difficult, farmers need to reduce the size of their pigs.

That doesn't mean the people running arts organizations are "pigs." Be careful how you interpret this. Most are sincere, passionate folks that truly love the art form they are helping. It's the size of the corporate structure that becomes the pig.

Here's an example: the Clearwater organization began as a small, community driven, music loving group that protected the Hudson River. As time went on, the pig got so big and fat that most of their attention was spent on raising money to feed the pig and NOT to protect the garden they were part of. Eventually, they cancelled the famous Clearwater Folk Festival to conserve funds to keep the pig fed. The folks at the office didn't *want* that to happen ... but it did. They've since adjusted and are back, thankfully.

By contrast, the WoodSongs broadcast is a theatre event with artists from around the world, produces 44 shows a year in front of several hundred people on a Monday night with a 30+ member crew, syndicated to 500+ radio stations plus American Forces Radio in 173 nations, a 5-camera HD-TV broadcast edited, closed captioned, satellite fed and viewable in 96M USA TV homes on public TV, live online feed plus over 800 shows archived for free on our website ... all on a weekly budget of $629.

How is this possible, you ask? Because ... *drum roll, please* ... we have a teenie weenie pig.

My point is simple: If the pig consumes more money than the artists in the garden ... *the pig must die.* Or at least go on a diet.

All arts careers, bands and groups need to take a close look at the condition of the garden you are part of. An organization with a flourishing garden and a little pig is doing it right. If you see your garden withering, struggling ... if the artists are frustrated and the audiences dwindling ...

... *take a close look at the pig.*
It might be time to trim some bacon

A packed WoodSongs broadcast at the Lyric Theatre

51

Tree Hugger

KayKay in the Korn Kave at the Kabin

If I'm known for anything, it's taking a pro-active stance on two things: I call myself a "folksinger" and I refer to myself as a "tree hugger." I've already explained the folksinger part in my other books, let's explain the tree hugger issue.

I must get 1,000 emails a year asking me, *"What exactly is a Tree Hugger, anyway???"*

Good question. I know to some it carries a bit of a political, eco-nazi image, but that is *not* what I mean by it nor is it my viewpoint. A heated argument about whether or not global warming is real or contrived is irrelevant to my views about using the phrase.

To me, a Tree Hugger is a peaceful, earth conscious person who enjoys a simpler, intelligent, artistic life. It's about the artists and the music they make, the food they grow and protection of their space on this earth.

It's about you, me, our children ... and our music.

Tree Huggers are folks who choose people over money, family over careers, dreams over reality, home cooked meals over fast food, a fireplace, homemade music and those who listen closely to the dreams of their children. We enjoy a hearty laugh, a good glass of red wine late at night, a hot cup of coffee in the morning. It's for anyone brave enough to bring a dream to life.

Tree Huggers work in the hope of making you a little happier, to get you to sing, and draw, and create. I don't care if it's music, art or cooking, so long as you're having fun. Life is too short to be worrying about half the stuff we fret over nowadays.

It's a sense of nature, a log cabin you built yourself and a walk in the woods in October. It's flannel pajamas on a snowy Appalachian night with the fireplace cracklin' all warm and cozy while reading a good book. It's a guitar, a poem, a song, a canvas, a sculpture, a dream and a vision all wrapped up together like a fresh baked batch of homemade cookies, ready to share.

Henry David Thoreau was a Tree Hugger, he just didn't know it at the time. Al Gore is a Tree Hugger that rides in limos and private jets. Me? I'm a Tree Hugger who lives with his kids in a Kentucky cabin and loves to play Martin guitars and my Vega banjo for folks.

A Tree Hugger simply loves life on a healthy planet Earth.

I love what the earth is here for, I love what it provides and respects how it does it. I believe the earth has a purpose and that mankind *(that word includes women)* has a purpose on it. And I believe that taking care of the earth, being a good steward of it, starts in your own hometown, in your own back yard.

"Trees are the earth's endless effort to speak to the listening heaven."
Rabindranath Tagore

LOVERS, HATERS, AWARDS & CRITICS

*Fact: Anyone attempting to create outside of the box
is a target for those incapable of the same effort.*

"The music on WoodSongs is good ... but the host is an idiot."
Grey Brendle, Beaufort, SC

And so goes a recent public post on a Facebook page from someone I don't know, never met and who hasn't a clue about me at all. Every now and then, these little verbal spears appear amid the accolades, praises, applause, standing ovations, awards-with-my-name-completely-misspelled and other genuine kindnesses. And it makes you wonder:

Why?

Not *"why am I an idiot."* Heck, maybe so and I haven't realized it yet. But why would someone you don't know say something so negetive so publicly about someone they've never met?

Garrison Keillor is a fine man who has created an otherwise impossible broadcast of *A Prairie Home Companion* and, aside from all the praise he receives, he was constantly BLASTED by those who thought he talked too much, can't sing, is a terrible writer, self inflated ego and on and on. All from folks who have never met him.

Chris Thile is one of the finest musicians on earth. A sincere fellow of indescribable talent. He is stepping into the golden shoes of Garrison as the new host of *A Prairie Home Companion* and, amidst the great reviews of his effort, I have read some of the most scathing comments about his impending failure, his "Garrison Wanna-Be" status and bone-crippling negativity of his hosting skills.

Mainly, it seems, from the same people who hated Garrison. Actually, they hate Garrison and hate Chris but evidently listen to the show every week for some reason in order to be qualified to make such horrid reviews regarding efforts they themselves are incapable of imagining, no less accomplishing. Even on a small scale.

So, again I ask ... Why?

Garrison and Chris do great work. The difference between those two gentleman and myself, aside from the shear stature of their accomplishments, is they are paid, I am not. I created and work on WoodSongs for free. I get nothing. Not a cent, ever. The crew works for free and the artists who come on the show do so for free. The show goes free to public radio, free to public television and I was able to arrange hundreds of complete broadcasts to be archived online that anyone can watch ... for free.

Heck, my hometown newspaper, even after all this work, all this music, all these events and all these years, can't even spell my name right on those very rare occasions that I am included in a story about projects that I create. Can't someone who volunteers to do something good ever catch a break?

One of my many misspelled awards, but still very much appreciated!

Evidently not. But that's ok.

All artists, dreamers, risk takers, poets and performers have a deep love for their craft. And they have an even deeper love for their audience. Presenting their creations to the scathing opinions of others is like showing your nakedness to people you already know don't like you.

Just consider the enormous amount of stress and pressure a project like WoodSongs would place on someone. Can you imagine doing 44 of these productions a year ... with virtually no money to operate on? Harsh criticism, especially in public, is the most disheartening, demoralizing thing in an artist's life ... and it can wound deeply.

The Truth about the Lie

It hurts ... until you realize a very simple, basic truth: haters are even more scared and more lonely than you are. They swim in a deep pool of insecurity and have such low self esteem that their only salvation is the self elevating illusion that comes from looking down on those they perceive accomplish more than they can.

I think, in the end, the words of harshness become irrelevant to the work at hand. Like any worthy endeavor the artist, creator or dreamer only achieves their goal by keeping their head down, their spirits up ... and band aids handy for the wounds that come from those critical of what they themselves are incapable of doing. Sometimes a critic can make you better, they can sharpen you like a blade against a stone. They can also rip into your spirit so deeply it makes you feel like quitting.

The point is nothing we do should be for any other reason than for the love of it. Love is the greatest motivation of the arts, and haters have no place in that world. They are, at best, jealous onlookers.

Recently a very good friend of mine, David McLean, came up with an idea of an award show that he himself couldn't be part of. I watched him get blasted from all onlookers ... at first. But he kept his chin up and didn't stop and now he is a hero. I'm proud of David. His

My star on the sidewalk of Lexington outside the Kentucky Theatre, both names misspelled. They offered to fix it but I told them to keep it as it is

heart proved more powerful than those who denied his efforts.

I'm sure Mr. Brendle is a fine fellow and I can sort of imagine him sitting in front of a TV watching WoodSongs muttering and throwing his popcorn at the TV set every time "that idiot" comes on the screen. And that's ok, because his harsh review means he's watching the ding-dang show, the very thing we all work so hard on, and for free, to accomplish. So in the end, we win ... not him.

It's just a shame the only thing I know of the gentleman is his public unkindness. Maybe, someday, Mr. Brendle will accomplish something so wonderful they will place a star along Main Street in his honor with both his names misspelled, too.

"It's a shallow life that doesn't give a person a few scars."
Garrison Keillor

"Never argue with the stupid or the foolish ... they will defeat you with experience."
Mark Twain

The BRONZE STAR

Several folks have written to ask about the bronze star I wear the lower part of my jacket.

My father, Michael, died about five days before I was born.

My stepfather, Bill, was a very fine man, but when I found out about my *real* dad things changed. Michael became a striking mystery that consumed me. As I grew up, I found I myself missing him greatly. I wished he was nearby, longed to know the sound of his voice and to stand in his shadow.

The very first male relative I met of my father's was my son, MichaelB when he was born and finally opened his eyes. I saw for the very first time a reflection of my own father. And now Caleb reflects that same light.

Eventually I went on a search for my dad's past and his family and finally found them. My cousin, Laddie, became very proactive in seeking out belongings and artifacts of my dad.

One of them was my father's bronze star.

I do not wear it on my chest, as the star is not mine. I put it on my lower jacket as a tribute to my father. I wear it, not as a military or political statement, but in honor of my father who earned it. It is a way of letting him be with me when I am on stage ... and I find it comforting.

ON STAGE: Me, my beautiful wife Melissa and my dad's bronze star that I wear on my jacket

I always wondered what our relationship would be like. Would he like me? Would he be proud of me? Would we be close as a father and son should be? What was the sound of his voice as he called my name?

All I know is this: if I was to leave this life I would hope my sons would love me enough to publicly remember me and be proud of me. So, this I am doing for my father.

My Father's Grave

Children need the ones they love to love each other.

A family is like a strong tower. It protects and nurtures kids, makes them feel both loved and lovable. It teaches little boys how to love a woman because they see their dad loving their mom. It teaches daughters how to care for a husband and family ... and how to be treated by a man ... because they see mom and dad being loving with each other

I talk about it on WoodSongs virtually every show. Moms and dads and families have got to find a way to stick together and make that family work.

Divorce affects a child much like the planes that slammed into the World Trade Towers. The damage is more severe than first observed. It burns their very soul - from the inside out. The horror is progressive, unyielding and moves onward beyond the observation of those who caused the injury. And eventually, often when the child is now an adult, the internal foundations that make them a whole person come crashing down into a massive pile of rubble.

My mom and real dad had a hard marriage. He was dying of cancer, they were separated and, five days before I was born, my dad died. The families polarized, didn't speak to one another and my mom quickly abandoned my father's side of the family after the funeral, ran off and remarried ten months later.

My father Michael, a few years before his passing

My mom and stepfather didn't seem to love each other, either. And I grew up hiding my brother and sister under beds at night during huge and often violent arguments.

I didn't know about my real father till I was 12, during one of those wall-smashing fights. I didn't carry his name, I knew nothing about him. Who was this man? Who was this mysterious new father?

And who on earth was this guy I thought was my dad all this time? I wasn't allowed to ask, so I let it go.

I stayed silent for several years as the confusion took root. I have learned that kids who grow up like this often gravitate to the very drama and unhealthy personalities they desperately want to flee from. And the planes that crashed into me as a kid burned. And my towers fell and my first marriage ended in rubble. When my second marriage failed, very much against and will, I went on a search for my real dad and his family.

I eventually found my cousin Laddie, who as a young boy was very close to my dad. He has kindly given me a wealth of photos and newspaper clippings and told me many stories that helped me know my father better. And he showed me a copy of the family tree that listed all the brothers and sisters and aunts and uncles of my dad's family.

And looking through all that material, when you come to the part of my dad and mom, to the part about me, there is simply a question mark and a note that says *"... name and location unknown."*

Wow. It wasn't intended to be that way, I know. But all I ended up being to me my dad's legacy was a "question mark."

Laddie and his lovely wife, who have been very kind and supportive, took me and MichaelB to my father's grave for the very first time. As we walked through the green grass past the headstones of hundreds of people in the cemetery in Forest Hills, NY my cousin finally pointed and said,

"There, Michael. There's your dad."

This was the closest I have ever been to my father. I was six feet away from being able to hold his hand and hear his voice and watch his eyes as he spoke to me. And I knelt over the grave and ran my fingers across his name on the family headstone. And every image of every fight and every moment of confusion and desperate thoughts of wondering

MichaelB and my dad

who I was and where did I fit and how much I completely needed this man crashed into me again.

And then everyone gave me a private moment, alone with my Father, for the very first time.

It was very hard and very emotional. And as I knelt down I took an oak leaf laying on the grass atop his grave as a keepsake of the moment and said my farewell. The wishful images of my dad playing baseball with me the way I play catch with my own son flashed through my head. The dream of my dad scuffing up the hair of my head with approval over something completely stupid I accomplished, the way I do for MichaelB and Caleb, danced across my eyes.

My heart was very heavy for my own children. I don't want those emotional planes burning inside their hearts, too. They deserve, need, so much better.

And as I walked away from my father, I was left wondering how different my life might have been if only the people I loved would have loved each other.

My father shaking hands with the Mayor of New York City, recieving his award as a highly decorated detective. To the right is his graduation photo as a police cadet

Artists & Krit-Icks, part 2

Recently a critic reviewed *The Dream*, my song about the Earth at peace recorded with a 61 piece symphony and four children's choirs singing in French, English, Spanish and Russian. I worked my butt off on it for almost a year. The album was getting rave reviews all over the country ... and then this reviewer got hold of it and gave it a horrible, personal, scathing review.

It rattled me. For a minute.

I write this because I think all of you, whether amateur songwriter, or professional, are incredibly talented, brilliant and beautiful in sprit. Never stop, even if it means getting pounded into the ground, ridiculed and having to climb up off your bloodied knees all the time.

Remember: The critic creates *nothing.*

So, I offer some words of wisdom for all artists to consider:

**"It is much easier to tear down than to build,
it takes less talent to scoff than to create,
it is the essence of laziness to be critical."**
Benjamin Disraeli

**"Far better it is to dare mighty things,
to win glorious triumphs even though checkered by failure,
than to rank with those poor spirits who neither enjoy
nor suffer because they live in the gray twilight
that knows neither victory nor defeat."**
Theodore Roosevelt

**"Twenty years from now you will be more disappointed
by the things you didn't do than by the ones you did.
So throw off your anchors. Sail away from safe harbor.
Explore ... Dream ... Discover."**
Mark Twain

The 911 call

Husband: *My wife is missing.*

Sheriff: *Height?*

Husband: *I'm not sure.*

Sheriff: *Weight?*

Husband: *Don't know.*

Sheriff: *Color of eyes?*

Husband: *Sort of brown I think.*

Sheriff: *Color of hair?*

Husband: *Kinda blondish*

Sheriff: *What was she wearing?*

Husband: *I didn't notice.*

Sheriff: *Was she driving?*

Husband: *Yes, my truck.*

Sheriff: *What kind of truck?*

Husband : *A 2016 pearl white Ram Limited 4X4 with 6.4l Hemi V8 engine ordered with the Ram Box bar and fridge option, led lighting, back up and front camera, Moose-hide leather, heated and cooled seats, climate controlled air conditioning. It has a custom matching white cover for the bed, Weather Tech floor mats. Trailing package with gold hitch, sunroof, DVD with full GPS navigation, satellite radio, Cobra 75 WX ST 40-channel CB radio, six cup holders, 3 USB port, and 4 power outlets. I added special alloy wheels and off-road Toyo tires. It has custom retracting running boards and under-glow wheel well lighting.*

Sheriff: *Don't worry, we'll find your truck.*

Tools of the Trade

I get asked a lot about the guitars I use on stage. Which is nice, it means folks are listening and noticing. They look like pieces of art. To me anyway. I love my instruments. So here you go:

My banjo is a custom made VEGA open-back long neck, designed by Greg Deering. It has a true, clean, golden tone. The Intellitouch NS Micro Banjo tuner is spectacular, it clips onto the head brackets and is the best I have found for banjos.

All my guitars are Martin 12-fret, wide neck models. Why the wide neck? Because of tone and clarity. When you play a chord on a regular guitar, Martin or otherwise, you hear the wash of the chord. With a wide neck, especially these, you strum the chord and actually hear the individual notes that make up the chord. I love that. And I love the classic look of the slot tuners.

I play only Martin guitars, I've always used them and will never change that. They are the best. In the past I preferred the 000-28s guitars. However, my pride and joy is the Martin QUAD, my very own signature model 0000-28s, pictured here. It is a finger-picking canon.

I use Martin Lifespan phosphor bronze 80/20 medium gauge strings. All have an Elliott capo that I leave on the nut of the guitar, I use NP2 brass finger picks and Goldengate large white thumb picks. The Intellitouch NS Micro tuner works great on acoustic guitars. I prefer a good, padded leather gig bag to a hard shell case. The best are made by Reunion Blues.

I protect my Martin guitars at all cost. Even at big venues I would stare union stage managers in the eye and say:

"Here's my Martin - and over there is my wife.
Don't EVER let me catch you messing with my Martin."

DIMENSIONS OF ART

It is the difference of seeing a Van Gogh online, verses seeing it in a museum. It is hearing music in your earbuds, verses watching the artist onstage. It's viewing the song on YouTube, verses singing to your family gathered in the living room on a winter night.

Real vs fake. Organic vs digital. Two dimensions vs three ... the great artistic war of the new century.

Years ago, all art was three dimensional. It captured all of your senses and immersed you in the baptism of another artists life and spirit. It wasn't reproduced, it was experienced. That is what art, true art, is for. This changed with the advent of two wonderful inventions: the *photograph* and the *record player.* Let me repeat: they are wonderful, but only when they (and their resultant offspring) are kept in their proper place.

The photograph, which morphed into television, computer screens, cell phones and iPads, captured a three dimensional soul ... whether a person or a mountain or a flower in a vase ... and relegated it down into the two dimensional world. In perfect form, this would inspire others to go out and experience the mountain, meet the person and smell the fragrance of that beautiful flower.

The same with records and radio. The musical arts once thrived in a three dimensional world of small stages and clubs and courtyards, front porches and living rooms. Soon, the art was captured and relegated down into the two dimensional world. In perfect form, and this often worked, the record and the radio would motivate the audience to learn that song or go see that artist in person.

Not anymore.

We are, for the first time in human history, dealing with a generation who experience art and music primarily in the two dimensional world.

And that's a shame. Kids today experience music in cheap $15 earbuds, computer speakers, smart phones, video screens, and a couple of speakers in a car speeding down a hiway. It has become a very rare thing for kids and families to see music performed in person. Venues, in this economy, are closing by the dozens and America is becoming venue starved. The opportunity for three dimensional art is becoming harder to find.

Even the "star system" is designed to remove art from you, selling you on the insane idea that only the "Star" is truly qualified to play music, therefore you are relegated down to a two dimensional participant. Your role is to buy the record. The farther the music industry can push you away from your own music, the better customer you become.

As the audience surrenders to the digital world, artists lose their ability to capture their attention as two dimensional art saturates the audience with an endless bombardment of mundane artist efforts.

Pete Seeger comes to mind. Again.

Pete released his records, went on TV when he could, got played on radio ... all in an effort to get the three dimensional world, his audience, singing. And it worked. He used the two-dimensional platform to stay connected to the real, organic three-dimensional audience.

But be forewarned: getting used to the flat-screen, digital world of art is not good. It robs you and your children of the organic thrill of being part of it. We have grown accustomed to the horrid sound of a low-res MP3 blaring from a mini-speaker on a smart phone.

The best role of the two dimensional media is to get real people involved with real art. The two dimensional media platforms are, as I said, very powerful tool to inspire. But not replace.

I try to do that with WoodSongs.

At the end of every show I try to encourage the audience to use what they just heard as inspiration to play their own music. Getting the audience to be proactive is the goal. That's why we started the Coffeehouse project and the Classroom program.

And that's what I hope you do. Get involved, become proactive. Get off your duff and paint, play, write, sing, create.

"In art, the hand can never execute anything higher than the heart can inspire."
Ralph Waldo Emerson

Use WoodSongs, successful as it is on radio, public television and online, as a wellspring of inspiration ... but then *turn it off* and play your own song.

The digital world is fine to introduce art, but assuming it is real is like trying to date the paper of a magazine centerfold. Instead, baptize your heart, soul and spirit in the magnificent world of three dimensional life.

It is like a wonderful paradise of music and art.

"Let us live the beauty of reality."
Charles Lamb

Poppy

It is snowing as I look out my cabin window tonight.

The woods feel so silent and still, the wind is just barely there, pushed away by the soft sounds of a fireplace in the next room. Without Melissa and the twins here, the house is very still, very pensive. So I am writing, and waiting.

Waiting. Waiting. Waiting for their return.

But I am torn with a lot of feelings tonight. A confusing tsunami of disappointment, regret, resignation ... and loss.

My mind is vivid with a technicolor memory of when I was still living in New York, long ago. Seventeen years old, sleeping on a cot in the attic of a friend's house by myself with everything I owned in a brown paper bag.

I had left home, supporting myself with a part time job at a grocery store. I would change the prices on shelf items with a can of Lysol and a steel wool pad, scrubbing the ink off and then stamp the new prices on. A couple years later that was all replaced by bar codes. But I was at my job this afternoon, an angry and ripped-to-shreds teenager that was put in a position to have leave his home.

I remember forcing myself to stay busy at my job. I needed the money now. I promised my friend I would pay rent for the little attic room. The feeling of that empty, hollow hurt in my chest is still there when I think back. I remember it very clearly. I was mad. I was scared. I was fed up.

And I was still just a kid.

I remember looking up and seeing the tall, husky figure of him as he walked down the store isle to me. I called him dad, but he wasn't. I found out just a few years ago that I had another dad who died before I was born. That little piece of information answered a lot of things for me. I could never figure out why I was always treated differently, why I never fit in. Then I found out my "dad" wasn't my dad. Although I carried this man's name publicly, but it wasn't really mine. I had two names: a public one and then a secret one that I could never say out loud. It made me not know who I was, or who I belonged to, or who I was supposed to be.

So I handled it all like I was still a kid.

Because I was.

And he walked up to me and asked how I was doing. And I said OK, too proud to ever look up. And he put his hand on my shoulder ... I don't ever recall he ever touched me before or after this day ... and said, *"Let's go to the diner next door for a hamburger."*

So, I put down my can of Lysol and my steel wool pad and left the store with him. That was OK, because, after all, this was his store and he gave me this part time job. And we sat at the diner counter and he didn't say much. I didn't say much. But he wanted to know if I was OK and he handed me some money in case I needed it.

And then he left.

That was the closest I ever felt to him. I wanted to run out of the diner and grab him and hug him. I knew he cared about me. I knew that, in his heart, he didn't see a difference if I was his or not. And if left to his own inclination, he wouldn't treat me any different than my brother, who was his actual son.

But he wasn't my dad. And I wasn't his son.

And it mattered to me that others reminded him of that constantly.

And soon I left.

I left New York and went as far as I could without leaving the nation and landed on the Mexican border in Laredo, Texas and began a search, a journey that finally led me through trials and errors and stupid mistakes. I would have given the world to have a father to help me navigate through it all.

That journey led me to Melody.

And Rachel.

And MichaelB.

And now Caleb and Makayla.

And I learned from the things I missed as a kid, and now try to be the best dad I can be for them. I tell them I love them constantly. They have a hug whenever they want, and when they don't expect it. I tell them that, someday, they will be in trouble. They might have done something bad that might even be their fault. They will be embarrassed or ashamed. And that's the day they will need their dad the most. And I will be there for them. No matter what. Always. And forever.

But tonight the snow is turning to ice. And the cold is creeping into the cabin and I really need to put a another log in that fire. But I won't move, I won't stop until I've finished writing.

Because when Poppy died I never got to say goodbye.

And I still feel bad about that. I didn't really know him that well and he never really knew me.

I saw him a few months before he passed and he was so frail, no longer the big husky Bull of a man I remember. I walked into the hospital room and he took my hand and he asked me how I was.

And for a moment, as I held his hand in that hospital bed, I was seventeen again. And scared. Living in an attic and angry and alone. But only for a moment. Because I'm not a kid anymore and times and people change.

Poppy gives his group hug to Melody and cousins Megan and Jazzy

Poppy is gone. He didn't reject me, I didn't reject him. Things just happened. Stupid things. I will forever miss the man who took me for a hamburger and sat with me that afternoon in a crummy diner. He was a good man, it meant the world to me that he did that ... and I never told him. And I will always regret that we never could get past what other people impugned on our relationship.

I needed him, but could never tell him.

Instead, I put all that energy into my children. They are the life and light and joy of my life. And I sit here tonight, mourning my stepfather's passing ... a man I really never knew very well. Writing in this cabin thinking of my children, and Melissa, and the twins.

Waiting. Waiting.
Waiting for their return.

"If I had a single flower for every time I think of you, I could walk forever in my garden."
Claudia Adrienne Grandi

CUTTING THE ARTS

It's a foolish thing to do although I do understand, with all due respect, that our leaders are trying to balance the books. I'm sure the waste alone in spending surpasses what we invest encouraging the arts. In turn, I'm sure the arts councils could do a better, more fair job at spreading the grants.

Having said that, I would hope our good government officials would consider the words of Winston Churchill: when considering cutting money for the arts in order to fund the war effort he said:

"Then what on earth are we fighting for?"

Whether Churchill actually said this or not is irrelevant. The point is simple, you can not provide a good place to live when the quality of life is not inspiring. Your hometown will not attract the

lucrative "creative class," a term I hate, if the creative atmosphere is barren. The arts are in fact an investment to attract families, tourism and entrepreneurs. It pays for itself many times over.

Re-directing how arts money is spent may be a wiser and more lucrative course, instead of cutting it. But that's a whole-nuther issue and nobody has yet asked my opinion.

Why I hate the term "creative class."

Simple: artists should never be separated from the spirit of their audience. Being an artist, making a living as one, comes from the grace and good heart of the audience. "Creative Class" somehow implies the artist is special, more blessed, more important than the audience that provides for them.

Bull-dinkies, I say.

An artist is best positioned as a servant, a laborer of heart and spirit underwritten by the audience that accepts their work.

I'll give you an example of why this class structure doesn't work: Michael Jackson, arguably an impressive talent, jumped the shark when he floated a statue of himself down the River Thames. Michael Jackson wasn't god-like because he was famous, rich or had a massive audience. He was a fragile, flawed, mortal person *exactly* like his audience. He would have been less lonely and a lot more stable if he viewed his position in a humble manner.

To quote Pete Seeger:
"It is better to have friends than fans."

There is a solution for communities, teachers and home school families who appreciate art but have their budgets decimated. I hope everyone reading this would consider becoming a member of the *WoodSongs Front Porch Association* as we send massive roots music education into classrooms and home school families. Free. I think the government and arts council might study what we are doing just to see how much good can be accomplished on so very little. Visit us at SongFarmers.org

For the People Woody

The creation of the Woody Guthrie Opera

How hard can it be?

I had never been to an opera before.

Never watched one on TV, never even listened to opera on the radio. An acquaintance of mine with intense classical training thought that was borderline criminal. So, off we went to see the opera *La Boheme,* considered one of the most popular operas in the world.

Now understand: I come from the folk singer, workboots, jeans and flannel shirt world. My brain is banjo-wired and my idea of a stage is a front porch with a couple dozen friends.

But this ... this was something else.

That night over 2,000 people crammed into the music hall in Cincinnati wearing gowns and all the men wore ties. Men with ties! At first I thought I stumbled into a insurance salesman convention.

So the lights dim and the music starts ... real musicians with real instruments. Then the actors came out, real singers with amazing voices. And the lights moved, and the sets moved, and the audience was in hypnotic rapture through the entire production.

Wow! says I.

This is like an orgasm of three-dimensional art. Spectacular!

I really like this artform. I want to be part of it. I should write my own opera.

How hard can in be? I thought.

Well, it's pretty ding-dang hard.

The Humming Method

I'm really good at composing and knowing how the finished piece should sound, it's just that I don't read music. I use what I refer to as the "humming method" of composition and arrangement. Once my song is written, if I hear a string section in my imagination, I will sit with someone who knows how to score arrangements and I will hum it to them. Literally. Each part, one at a time.

I discovered this incredible music notation software called Sibelius. You use a piano keyboard, hook it up to a computer with the Sibelius software and start composing. You can write the cello line, and it will play it back to you as a cello sample. Viola and violin, same thing. When you play it back you are actually hearing how the string quartet, or horn section, or harp, or voices will sound.

It's kind of odd, actually. When I write a song on my couch I hear the finished record in my head, much like a painter sees the completed canvas in his head before he even puts brush to paint. Adding string sections, quartets, horns and classical touches to my music is not foreign to me. I recorded *The Dream* album with a 61-piece orchestra that way. I wrote the quartet arrangements for my *Walden* album, and long used string sections on the *WoodSongs* broadcast.

But an opera ... Could I really pull this off? And can I ever learn what all those Italian words mean? And what would my opera be about? Why, the most important folk song in the history of music, of course. A song so famous yet tethered to a bone crunching, dramatic story virtually unknown to the public.

A perfect, powerful opera ...

So I set about the task of actually composing a full, traditional opera about one of the greatest ... albeit unknown ... stories in American music.

The day Woody Guthrie began writing *This Land Is Your Land*.

The Libretto:
On February 23, 1940, the world is at war.

It was a cold, winter day in early 1940.

It was February 23, and a songwriter hunkered down in his small New York City apartment, grateful to be home, sitting in front of a small heater by his window with his lyric pad and guitar in his lap, finishing the lyrics to a new song.

You see, the young folksinger had just returned home from a job in the Pacific northwest writing a batch of songs for a documentary about the Grand Coulee Dam. He made his way south to Texas for a visit with his estranged wife and children, where he decided to divorce and leave them for good.

As he made his way back to his apartment in Greenwich Village in New York City to be with his new girlfriend, he ran out of money. First he sold his guitar. Then, finally, he sold his car and began hitchhiking.

He made his way as far as Pittsburgh and got caught in a cold, icy snowstorm. The winds blew right through him as he walked along the highway, hoping for a ride. Soon, the freezing cold overtook him, his body temperature began dropping and he started to feel faint.

A Pennsylvania Ranger happened along and found the songwriter suffering from near hypothermia, gave him a ride to his home where he fed him a bowl of hot clam soup and gave him money for a bus ticket home.

This generosity had a profound affect on the young songwriter. He considered the beauty of the roads and country he just traveled, the ribbon of a highway he just hitched rides on to make his way home. It clashed with what he was hearing on the radio

God Bless America

On the radio was song written by Irving Berlin called *"God Bless America"* which offended and angered the troubled singer. Actually, Woody hated that song to his core. He felt it was making fun of what was really happening to people in the country.

America readied for war. Nations are in the midst of a global economic meltdown and hundreds of able-bodied men were standing in soup lines across the country. Hitler is slaughtering millions of people in Europe, and influenza was killing millions more. The midwest is crippled by climactic changes that make "global warming" seem like a bad breeze, displacing hundreds of thousands of families into California for jobs promised but never realized.

There was every reason to be troubled, every reason to be angry, every reason to revolt over what was happening. And yet the the families of this land, folks like the Pennsylvania Ranger, were still so kind and passionate for each other. Their dignity superseded the troubles they faced.

Woody felt the Irvin Berlin song, as sung by the very operatic Kate Smith, made light of the true spirit, integrity and love of the average person. Every time he heard it on the radio he would erupt in anger. He felt people needed a song that reflected their true goodness and love for this land. As he made his way home on the bus, the ticket provided for him by the kindness of the Pennsylvania Ranger, he began writing the words to a song in retaliation to Irvin Berlin's tune.

It was his *anti-Irvin Berlin* protest song. His song would be called *"God Blessed America"* based completely on his communist view of society. Now, keep in mind, I'm not promoting communism here, I'm just telling a historic event.

See, back in the 1930's and 40's communism was just another American political party. They had candidates for President and had a large national following. Based on the bible account of the Apostles collecting material goods from the congregations and then redistributing them equally amongst the believers, communism had that same "share the wealth" doctrine ... which appealed to Woody and other poor, broke artists. That's why so many singers, actors and poets were communists back in those days. It seemed very cost effective.

Of course, Communism failed because, well, there's no money in it. But in Woody's day, it was "pre-Russian" so still somewhat acceptable. And so, his song *"God Blessed America"* was written decidedly from his communist beliefs.

Because of the kindness of that Ranger, Woody began composing the song. During the icy bus ride home, he began writing and, once he made it back to his apartment on February 23, 1940, he write down the lyrics to one of the greatest songs in America history.

And then pretty much forgot about it.

This Land Is FREE ... as in "FREE."

About seven years later his friend, the banjo player, fellow communist and folksinger Pete Seeger, was looking through Woody's book of lyrics and found the song. He liked the tune, lifted from an old Carter Family melody, but didn't like the title. Too "past tense" he said. So, Woody got a pencil, crossed out the original title and scribbled in the new one, *This Land Is Your Land."*

Woody never performed his song in public. He soon became quite ill and eventually was hospitalized, his body deteriorating from an inherited family disease. It was up

God Blessed America
This Land Was made for you + me
This land is your land, this land is my land,
From the California to the New York island,
From the Redwood Forest, to the Gulf stream waters,
God blessed america for me.

to his friends Pete Seeger, Joan Baez, the Kingston trio, Judy Collins and others to sing the song to the public. Actually, it became one of Pete Seeger's favorite concert songs because the whole audience would jump right in an sing the chorus.

By the late 1950's two very odd things happen:

a) Sen. Joe McCarthy went on an anti-Communist man hunt

b) Woody Guthrie's manager, who used to be a song plugger for Irving Belin oddly enough, decided to give *This Land Is Your Land* away to schools ... for free. It was a bold move, as this was the era of sheet music, and writers made most of their money from the sheet music sales of their songs. Giving it away for free was, well, stupid.

Or was it?

Before anyone could realize it, millions of kids began singing Woody Guthrie's song in classrooms, then festivals, then coffee houses. Giving away the song for free made people find out about Woody Guthrie, and then sheet music to all of his other songs began selling like crazy. The US Congress even considered making the song replace the harder-to-sing *Star Spangled Banner.*

Imagine that.

Millions of kids were singing the *pro*-communist *This Land Is Your Land* anthem across America at the height of the *anti*-communist activities ... and nobody realized it was a communist song.

Now that, I thought, *was an Opera.*

So, can a Folksinger compose an Opera?

Woody: For the People
is a traditional opera that merges
the classical audiences with the
huge folk and roots music world.

The answer is "Yes."

The opera is set in February 1940 as Woody is making his way back home. The dust bowl, the war, the depression is raging across America. The main characters are Woody, Pete Seeger and Paul Robeson. In real life they were good friends.

The overture, arias and librettos were written on a guitar and banjo in my cabin. I literally hummed the parts of each instrument as a musical scribe would write the arrangements down. Quickly, the musical story of Woody's majestic song began to take shape and on a sound stage of the University of Kentucky, the *Woody Guthrie Opera* burst to life with a full symphony orchestra and brilliant opera singers.

It was a hard as I thought it was ... but we got it done.

The recording session of the arias for the Woody Guthrie Opera, released on a CD album and viewable online at WoodyGuthrieOpera.com

Believe

From the Woody Guthrie Opera

Words & Music
©Michael Johnathon/RachelAubreyMusic/BMI
Performed in the key of G

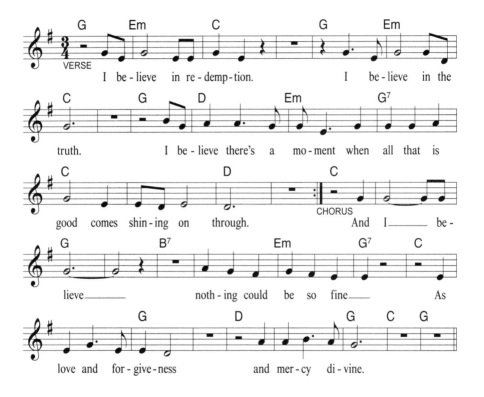

VERSE
I be-lieve in re-demp-tion. I be-lieve in the truth. I be-lieve there's a mo-ment when all that is good comes shin-ing on through.

CHORUS
And I_____ be-lieve_____ noth-ing could be so fine_____ As love and for-give-ness and mer-cy di-vine.

78

Believe is a good example of a song pre-opera stage. The CD shows how I originally wrote it. The humming method was used for the operatic arrangements later.

At the end of Act I, Woody is in a cafe with Pete, Paul and the Pennsylvania Ranger. He hears *"God Bless America"* on the radio. Woody is incensed and says he doesn't believe in that song. Pete asks, *"What do you believe?"*

This aria is Woody's answer ...

I believe in redemption
I believe in the Truth
I believe there's a moment
when all that is good
comes shining on through

I believe in transition
I believe change is good
It's the steady confusion of life
that transforms us from old into new

And I believe ... nothing could be so fine
As Love and Forgiveness ... and Mercy Divine

I believe in remorse
that forgivness is Truth
And that nothing else matters
as much as the love
between me and you

And I believe ... nothing could be so fine
As Love and Forgiveness ... and Mercy Divine

The Dream

The
Dream
Michael Johnathon

A folksinger, a song about the Earth at peace,
and a 61-piece symphony orchestra

**"If art is to nourish the roots of our culture,
society must set the artist free to follow his vision wherever it
takes him. We must never forget that art is a form of truth."**
John F. Kennedy

The Dream is a song, the title cut of my album.

It is one of the hardest artistic projects I've ever pulled off. In my heart it was almost like giving birth ... and I'm not saying I understand what it is like for a woman to bear a child. Not even close. But to me, in my world, in my heart it was close. It was painful, fearful, agonizing ... followed by shear exhilaration and pride when it was over.

To be honest, it was like giving birth to a rhino with the horn still attached.

The poetry is about our earth at peace. I wanted the song to be as majestic, powerful and universal as the concept of peace itself. It has four children's choirs singing in English, French, Spanish and Russian. The center piece of the song is when they all sing in their native languages but in unison. It is followed by the musical explosion of a 61-piece symphony orchestra.

Which brings me to the COVER ART, but before I explain that you should really listen to the song first, which is why I included it on the CD that comes with this book. And don't listen to it on a crummy pair of $10 earbuds, either. I worked hard on this. Listen to it loud on a good stereo with good speakers because there is a lot going on during this recording.

> **"Art is not what you see,
> but what you make others see."**
> *Edgar Degas*

It is not my intention here to be political, but to speak as an artist. To me, the world is saturated with beige-minded, vanilla-thinking, boring, common, unadventurous "stay-between-the-lines" art. As the marketplace of the music world shrinks and even disappears, songwriters and artists shrink back with it, careful not to take too much of a stand, careful not to rattle too many cages, careful not to alienate what is left of their little marketplace.

I mean, think about it:

Where are the songs against war? Where are the songs against terror? Where is the anthem that proclaims black lives do indeed matter? Where are the songs that decry violence against our police? Gone are the days of *We Shall Overcome, Masters of War* and *Where Have All the Flowers Gone.*

If they are out there, you don't hear them because even radio is hesitant to speak in that voice. Remember what happened to the Dixie Chicks?

Silence of the fearful condones the actions of the cruel.

Oh, I don't blame them, after all we have families to feed, rent to pay and as society restricts freedoms and rewards those who stand down instead, art will often "stand down" with it. But art shouldn't be that timid. Or shy.

When the collection of the songs for *The Dream* album were sequenced and I sat in the studio alone in the dark and listened for the first time to all the compositions in order, I began to envision the jacket art. It kept me up at night for days as it consumed the theatre in my mind.

The title song was about the earth at peace ... but the *truth* is the earth is *not* at peace. Years ago, album art was a powerful part of music. I remember as a kid being consumed with Steppenwolf's cover of an army of mice, the smudged makeup on Don McLean's thumb on *American Pie*, all the faces on *Sgt. Pepper*.

Those LP covers sucked me deep into the music.

Then music shrunk down from an LP to a CD, print became so small you can't read it and artists began to lose their imagination. Now, everybody downloads and there is no cover art at all. Most covers gives you the standard artist posing in front of a woodshed. Or posing in a field. Or posing wherever. Boring. Here's a news flash: I have never released a CD with my picture on the cover.

"Art is the lie that enables us to realize the truth."
Pablo Picasso

So I wanted this cover to be special, powerful, a statement. I created it to be an anti-statement to the song, so the song would have power. I wanted the jacket art to show visually what the song was hoping for musically. When I first showed the album jacket to Melissa, her reaction was to love it first followed by concern ... she didn't want to twins to ever see it.

That was good, actually. *The Dream* is not for kids because children are the peacemakers. It is for grownups, the ones actually causing all the violence.

The *outside* cover reflects the gentle hope of the song. The Earth: majestic and beautiful, distant and close, incredible and mysterious.

But the *inside* ... the inside is about the truth. It deploys the explosive anger that we destroy ourselves, our culture, yes, even our children with. It is graphic, brutal and, sadly, accurate.

Here is a response card we got from a radio DJ. This person saw the cover and made a judgement about the album and me without even listening to the song. I love our community of radio friends but *please notice this coward didn't even sign their name.* My name is on my album. It is *my* statement, I am proud of it and I stand by it openly. This wanker is hiding behind anonymity like a dork.

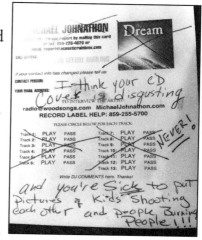

Yes, the cover art has terrible things children are doing to each other, as taught by violent, horrible adults. *The Dream* has four children's choirs asking, pleading for this to stop. This DJ didn't get it. I bet they have no problem watching this kind of horror in their living room over cornflakes as they watch CNN in the morning. I bet they watched planes crash into buildings, pulverizing thousands of people alive as the building fell. I bet they watched it over and over on their TV set. I bet they watched a woman get crushed to death followed by others dancing around her body as their children sat with them on the couch watching the *Wizard of Oz.*

I bet they have a golden murder weapon hanging around their neck and kiss it whenever they pray, too.

Some people think *The Dream* is a musical prayer for peace. It is not. It is actually a song about God asking US to stop it. It's God's prayer to mankind, not the other way around. It not a religious song, it is a song, a request, about protecting this wonderous creation by the one who created it to the ones he created.

**"It takes an artist with heart to make beauty
out of things that makes others weep."**
Clive Barker

Destroy the Box

So to all my fellow artists, I implore you:

Start thinking like an artist. Don't think outside the box ... *destroy* the box. Don't write a few songs and slap them on a boring CD and expect people to be moved. The world is saturated with the mundane. We are drowning in an ocean of beige. Be brave. Shake and rattle and crush. Make people react, feel, object, laugh, weep and cry. Be bold and fearless. Take risks and jump into the deep end of your soul to see what lies at the bottom. Invest in yourself, take chances with yourself ... because if you won't no one else will, either.

"Creativity takes courage."
Henri Matisse

And if you ever get a burr up your britches and send hate mail to someone, at least put your name and address on the ding-dang thing.

**"Every artist dips his brush in his own soul,
and paints his own nature into his pictures."**
Henry Ward Beecher

"Art is a revolt against fate."

Andre Malraux, France

THE DREAM

Give me a day, when the sun is shining
Give me a day, when the rain don't fall
Give me a day, when the city is singing
And then I'll cry, a long , hard cry

Give me a night, alone in the darkness
Give me a night, at my true love's side
Give me a night, when my children are dreamin'
And then I'll cry, a long, hard cry
(Noche en paz "Peaceful night"-SPANISH)

Give me a dream, that I wanna keep dreamin'
Give me a dream, I can fly through the sky
Give me a dream, all the people are dreamin'
And then I'll cry, a long, hard cry
(Miechta "Dream"-RUSSIAN)

Give me a war, where the people keep living
Give me a war, where the innocent survive
Give me a war, where the leaders are learning
And then I'll cry, a long, hard cry

Give me a tear, from the joys of laughter
Give me a tear, of a happy day
Give me a tear, of the peace that we're after
And then I'll cry, a long hard cry
And then I'll cry, a long, hard cry
(La larme du monde "Teardrop from the eyes of the world")
(La Paix "Peace"-FRENCH)

THE HAND photo taken during World War I on a battlefield in northern France where 1,357,000 French soldiers and 1,773,700 German soldiers died. *(STF/AFP/Getty Images)*

The 26 Commandments
for Artists ❧ Musicians

Art is a life mission, not a vocation.

Music must be a major part of your life
before it can become your livelihood.

If the audience doesn't respond,
take a hint and do something musically different.

Doing something different doesn't mean you are giving up on a dream;
it means you are stepping out of the way of an oncoming train.

Be original; if you are copying something already successful
you are being annoying.

If you are doing something original
you are also probably being annoying.

Love is the greatest transaction of the arts;
don't focus on money.

The audience is the greatest benefactor of the arts;
show them love and they will show you the money.

Be at peace with failure;
it is a stepping stone to success.

Success is an illusion and has nothing to do with real life.

Being popular is a drug; it often means you have simply
achieved the lowest common denominator and isn't
necessarily something you should be proud of.

Your instrument is an extension of your heart,
not your hands.

Critics are incapable of achieving what they are judging.
Ignore them.

Being in tune is more important than playing perfectly.

Never edit-in the sound of an audience that didn't show up.
It's called "lying."

Own your dream;
others will support anything they are not liable for.

Be honest; be fair; be motivated; be patient.
Each is a building block that will eventually house your dream.

Your dream is a carpet of stars floating in the universe before you;
keep your carpet clean.

Forgiving someone's mistake will make them more loyal to you.

The audience is the greatest benefactor of the arts;
view them as hearts, not wallets.

Invest in yourself;
if you don't, no one else will want to, either.

Accept the true size of your audience;
sometimes they are simply on your front porch or living room couch.
Don't be ashamed of their location.

Be humble and truthful with yourself by accepting the true reach of
your influence; being effective in your hometown is better than being
a non-existant ghost in the national consciousness.

Your CD is your business card ... give it freely.

You get paid if you develop an audience;
if you don't have a audience, don't complain if you aren't getting paid.

"Free" works. Use it wisely.

bonus commandment:
Don't waste your time on the uninterested

ARTISTS
who present other
ARTISTS
become better
ARTISTS

"My purpose in performing is to communicate the joy I experience in living."
John Denver

I love performing.

I love the magic of singing to an audience and watching their response. It doesn't matter if it's a theater, a coffeehouse, a living room concert or a front porch. It is a wonderful moment and I crave it. It is akin to picking flowers and handing them to your lover and basking in her response. Music, in its most organic form, is one of the greatest gifts and, in turn, rewards in human life.

Music is also the ultimate do-it-yourself occupation.

Most artists are self-employed and even run their own little record labels. Since the last of the music store chains died, performing is really the only way artists have to present their music to new audiences. The days of getting signed to a record company, releasing an album, getting it played on radio and followed by a big concert tour are over.

So, focusing on reality is important, spending precious moments on true action is critical. It applies to life in general, but most especially to music and art. In other words: don't just read about a garden ... turn off the TV, go outside and plant the ding-dang thing. Same with music: don't just listen to it on a smart phone, pick up an instrument and play it. Don't wish for it ... do it.

Don't whine there's no place to play ... get off your flabby duff and *create* a place to play.

What a great principle live by. Folks waste so much time dreaming about things they want to do. They think about it too much and before you know it, that clock ticks and the time to have accomplished it is gone. There is only so much young in the bank ... it gets spent with or without our participation.

Remember my previous reference to Van Gogh?

There is a huge difference between seeing a *real* Van Gogh painting in a museum verses seeing it on a computer screen. Online it sure looks beautiful ... but in person you stand in the spiritual presence of the artist himself, your eyes watch the direction of each brush stroke, your emotions ride every joy and pain the artist felt as he selected his colors. Seeing a Van Gogh in person is overwhelming because you are physically experiencing the life force and spirit of the artist himself.

It's the same with music.

Sure, you can hear the song in your earbuds and be excited and moved by the music, but watching the artist onstage you can be transported by the sheer emotion of the performance and by the crowd.

We live in a world saturated with musicial noise yet deprived of art. Today fans are emailed an MP3 of a song, they Google the band, YouTube the band, iTunes the band, download the band ... and they're done. Never even saw the band live.

That's why so many performance clubs and theaters are shutting down. America is becoming venue-starved because so many have surrendered to the two-dimensional world. The opportunity to experience three-dimensional art is becoming harder to find. Two-dimensional art saturates people with an endless bombardment of mundane efforts, making the public numb to even the idea of art.

Presenting other Artists builds your own Audience

At the end of every WoodSongs broadcast I try to encourage the audience to use what they just heard as inspiration to play their own music. I've put this into action with a project called the WoodSongs Coffeehouse.

We ask the audience and artists to consider using their homes, a barn, a local school basement or existing coffeehouse or club and, once a month or whenever suits them best, host a concert.

Most *WoodSongs Coffeehouses Concerts* are simple gatherings and most often happen in a host's living room. They invite 15 or 20 friends for music and a potluck dinner and pass the hat for the artist. You would be amazed at the high caliber of musicians on tour out there who would bend over backwards to get the gig.

I even wrote a *WoodSongs Coffeehouse How-To Manual* (free to anyone) You can start a music coffeehouse in your own backyard and WoodSongs will help you do it. There are scores hometown *WoodSongs Coffeehouses* operating across north America.

Our WoodSongs Coffeehouse in Germany is run by a fine songwriter Dieter Stoll. He and his group of friends started in a small barn they converted into a theatre. It is thriving and they were even featured on national German television. And newspapers. And radio.

Now think about that: our musician friends in Germany started a concert series that presents other artists ... yet *they* were featured on national television.

It's what I've been preaching about. Doing good work, even if for free, is the best PR campaign for any artist. You think they would have been featured on national television sitting around hoping to get discovered?

They got to work, they got creative ... and now they are reaping the reward of national recognition.

Understand the formula now?

It's impressive how much media attention artists that present other artists get. Our songwriter friends in Connecticut, Arkansas and across America that start a WoodSongs Coffeehouse ... a simple, mini hometown concert series ...enhance their reputations, endear themselves to their circle of fellow performers, attract a crowd and increase the size of their own audience.

Our SongFarmers Chapters are experiencing the exact same thing. I'll explain that next.

The stage of our
WoodSongs Coffeehouse
in Germany

"Happiness is a guitar, a microphone, a duet partner, a great venue, and an attentive audience!"
Dieter Stoll, WoodSongs Coffeehouse in Kusterdingen, Germany

We have nearly 100 *WoodSongs Coffeehouses* around the world presenting small concerts in their hometowns. The one in Dalton Georgia regularly has 300 or more at each concert event. They are held in cafes and living rooms, community centers and schools, book stores and cafes. The one in Las Vegas, Nevada is held in a converted auto mechanics shop, nicknamed the "Garage Mahal."

If you love music, especially if you are an artist and musician, I invite you to start a hometown concert series. It can be as simple as a house concert in your living room or a converted barn like Dieter uses in Germany. It doesn't matter where.

Just go to WoodSongs.com, click on the *Coffeehouse* button and we will help you. It's free.

Start a hometown
SongFarmer
MUSIC CHAPTER

Turn a Front Porch into a Stage ...

Alrighty, let's not get confused here:

A *WoodSongs Coffeehouse* is a homeown concert series with tickets, a way to help artists find an audience, sell their CDs and make a little money.

A *SongFarmers Music Chapter* is different. It's a gathering of friends, a musical picking jam. A place to bring people together as a musical community to pick, sing, learn and share. It's free.

One involves money, the other does not.

Let me make the case for a SongFarmers Music Chapter by stating a brutal fact:

FACT: Money will limit the size of your audience.

It's true. The more you try to get paid, the smaller your audience will become, defeating the effort to get paid. Where there is an audience, there are wallets and ... well, you can figure out the rest.

"He is richest who is content with the least
for contentment is the wealth of nature."
Socrates

Freedom is best cradled in the arms of contentment. We are sold on the idea that "stardom" and selling millions of albums is the goal of making it in the music business. Yet, all too often, those who "made it" are unhappy, frustrated and miserable.

Why? Because they overreached their ability to be happy.

Maybe the stage you seek is not an arena. Maybe it's a quiet moment playing alone in the woods, or on a front porch with your friends and family. It could be as powerful as performing to a group of school kids, bringing a joyful moment to residents at an old folks home or welcome distraction to a cancer ward in a hospital.

There is so much you can do with music that has nothing to do with "business." And, oddly enough, that's the best business model for all musicians to follow.

"Music is the art of the prophets that calm the the soul; it is one of the most magnificent gifts God has given us."
Martin Luther

Twenty thousand people screaming in an arena isn't "calm." Paying $100 or more for a ticket isn't exactly calming either. Sure, in its place it's fun. But sunsets, front porches in the rain, fireplaces when it snows ... now that's the stage for real organic, rural music. This is the music America was built on, families were built on, homes and communities were built on.

Let's turn the clock back a bit, let's build a front porch around the world together and calm things down.

Remember everything I've already said about the changes in the music business. The truth is you are not Bob Dylan, you are not Garth Brooks and you are most likely going to be a wonderful song-writer with a day job.

There is nothing wrong with that.

Now that we've gotten that out of the way: what do you do with all that passion, heart, music and song? Before you can step forward into a new path, you have to accept the destination.

For most folks, that would simply be: Joy. Joy in life, joy in the size of your audience. Joy in who your audience actually is.

"I would rather sit on a pumpkin and have it all to myself, than be crowded on a velvet cushion."
Henry David Thoreau

That's why I encourage everybody to gather your friends once a month or so, pick up an instrument, play three chords and the truth, and turn your living room couch into the greatest stage in the world.

How To Start ... it's Free

It was a great suggestion made during our first WoodSongs Gathering ... a simple picking jam and song swap of friends on a regular basis in your living room, front porch, local coffeehouse even a school room.

Join dozens of SongFarmer Clubs across America, we even have one in the Virgin Islands. They are bringing neighbors and friends together to pick, sing and share community friendship. It's simple:

First: become an active member of the WFPA. The folks who attend don't have to be members, although that would be nice. Only the organizer.

Second: create a Facebook page that looks like this: "SongFarmers of (your hometown)" and link to SongFarmers.org

Your SongFarmers gatherings should always be free, non-ticketed, pot luck and involve as many kids as you can. One of the amazing things about these clubs is discovering the vibrant seedling community of young players. It is amazing, it's easy, and it's fun.

Start your own!

Contact us by sending an email to WFPA@WoodSongs.com and we will send you logos and artwork you can use to start your own SongFarmers Music Chapter. There's more info on the website SongFarmers.org

"Without music, life would be a mistake."
Friedrich Nietzsche

Our first SongFarmers Chapter

There's nothing more lonesome than the sound of a perfectly good front porch with no music on it.

SONG FARMERS OF SHELBY COUNTY APRIL 17TH 5 PM

STRAND THEATRE

SONG FARMERS OF SHELBY COUNTY APRIL 17TH 5 PM

Our SongFarmers Chapter in Shelby County Indiana held an event in a local theatre

The SongFarmers Chapter in Tellico Plains TN in the cabin home of Perry Brake

SongFarmers
Jamming Tips

1- TUNING: It's ok if you are not sure how to tune your instrument, others will help you. Being in tune is better for you, your instrument and the group.

2. TUNE OFTEN: You are not being distracting or rude! Tuning should be done before you play your first song and you can easily check your tuning between songs and tweak when necessary.

3. TIMING: This is the speed and tempo of the song. If you're not sure of the tempo try to focus on the bass player. The Bass player drives the tempo of the song. This is a fun thing to learn. Remember as songs become louder, they tend to become faster. Just follow the song leader and you will be just fine.

4. SONG SELECTION: A SongFarmer event is a community effort. There are no "stars" at a SongFarmer jam, everyone is equal. That means we want to pick songs that the group can play together. We want everyone to have fun!

5. SONGS WITH LYRICS help the players notice chord changes easier. Tunes with no words - instrumentals - are generally more difficult for a group to play.

6. SONG KEY: This is usually the first chord of the song. Tell the group what KEY your song is in so the group can join in. Remember: simple is best.

7. SING FROM THE HEART: Nothing about a SongFarmers Music Chapter is about "perfection," it's about love, joy, community and music. If you are doing a song like *This Land Is Your Land* invite the other singers to join you on the chorus. Even if you don't play an instrument you can still sing and be a SongFarmer!

8. VOLUME: If you can't hear the lead singer you are probably playing too loud. The harder you use the instrument the quicker it will go out of tune.

Our goal in a SongFarmer event is to make everyone else have
fun and sound better. The more you consider others the more you will shine.
Your fellow SongFarmers will appreciate it ... so have fun!

Prepared by Perry Brake
SongFarmers of Tellico Plains, Tennessee

Good friends PICK together, they don't pick ON each other.

That is the beauty of simple, organic, rural music.

Ready. Aim. Pick.

SongFarmers.org

The world is very angry ... but we don't have to be.

Have you ever considered that musicians are the greatest soldiers of peace in the world? People don't fight when they listen. People don't argue when they listen.

Musicians get people to stop. And listen ... and feel. That's why using music for things other than trying to sell albums is so very important. Have you ever picked up your guitar and made a four song visit to a battered women and children's shelter? Or a children's ward in a burn unit? Performing for aged folks in a retirement home will bring your heart payment far greater than anything you can put in your wallet.

BMI, ASCAP & SESAC
must change their business model because
Artists are no longer free to be artists.

"If art is to nourish the roots of our culture, society must set the artist free."
John F. Kennedy

ONCE UPON A TIME, music was everywhere. It wasn't just entertainment. It was community, family, friends, fun and a sense of humanity. But what happened?

Music went from the Front Porch into stores and bins. Now the "bins" are gone, and so is the sense of community. Part of the loss has been the closing of thousands of music venues ... stages for artists to meet their audience.

Part of the destruction of the music business has been the over-use, the over-reach of licensing music. This is a delicate subject, easily misunderstood. So let's start with this thought:

"A bird doesn't sing because it has an answer, it sings because it has a song."
Maya Angelou

You have a song ... but you are not free to sing it anymore.

In the early days, before corporate America figured out how to sell vibrating air on round vinyl discs, people were free to sing wherever they wanted. Cafes and street corners, sidewalks and theatres, schools and bars ... anywhere.

This was the musical garden that gave birth to great art. Music "birds" like Bob Dylan, Woody Guthrie, Pete Seeger, Joan Baez, Judy Collins all began their careers by meeting their audience on simple, common stages.

Maya Angelou's little birds are not so free to sing anymore. Those birds are only allowed to sing on government approved stages licensed by BMI, ASCAP or SESAC.

**Woody Guthrie singing on a city sidewalk in 1943;
today illegal without a license**

**Woody Guthrie singing in a small bar for tips;
today illegal without a license**

Music in a small town General store ... today illegal without a license

Any fee that prevents an artist from reaching the audience has no value.

The world of the arts has changed, my friends. America has become a venue starved nation. The business model of music has changed. Arts venues can thrive, flourish and make a living for many good folks ... when it's done right.

But the world of arts needs to stop focusing on money because the audience, the source of the money, could care less. They want heart, passion and spirit. Whenever an arts endeavor launches as a "money enterprise" it is doomed for failure.

That sounds anti-capitalistic and I don't mean it that way. My point is the business plans most are using are outdated, poorly executed and all wrong.

Mus♪cVenues MATTER

SongFarmers.org

Many great venues across America have closed the past couple years because of poor business plans, an over focus on money ... or because of outdated licensing practices.

In my area alone venues like the Rudyard Kipling, Jim Porters and several others have shuttered their doors leaving the music public and the artist community in their wake. I bet you know of many in your area that have disappeared as well.

One thing that most groups can change for the better is the size of their Pig. Remember the Pig?

Another change that is needed *desperately* is regarding BMI, ASCAP and SESAC, called **"Performing Rights Organizations"** or **"PROs."** These agencies do wonderful work to collect royalties for artists from radio airplay, live performance of songs and more

The PROs have a great history of being a huge help to artists, big and small, new and established. I remember when I was just starting out, Clay Bradley at BMI in Nashville went through a great effort to explain how things worked in the music world when I knew absolutely nothing. Clay was very kind, helpful and spent all the time that was needed until I was able to get things through my thick little noggin'.

Let me make this clear:
I like BMI, ASCAP and SESAC

I just want them to change the way they are licensing music venues. It is outdated and no longer helpful to the artists they claim to be helping. The system they are using now began in the 1940's and worked ok for awhile. Then about 1995 the music business began its slide downward. The internet and free downloads reared its head and the financial structure of the music world collapsed with it.

Everyone is changing with the times ... except the PROs. They continue to use the antiquated formulas of music licensing, once a great help to artists. Today it acts like a gun to their head.

It works like this:

PROs charge the venue a licensing fee to present music in their establishments and, in turn, pay royalties to the artists who have their songs performed in those clubs

In theory, anyway.

Fact: Most artists who play 1,000 seat-or-less venues don't see a penny from the PROs. I'm not picking on the PROs here, just stating a brutal truth.

Fact: Venues are the gateways between artists and the audience, the venue operators are the soldiers in the war to find that audience ... and the current business model is killing them off.

Fact: unless a venue has a license **it is illegal for them to let any artist perform in their room.**

**A small concert in a private home with an artist playing
their own songs ... illegal without a license**

101

How Hard Can It Be?

Artists are no longer free to be artists so BMI, ASCAP and SESAC should either help them or get out of their way.

Little clubs, farmer's markets, schools and coffeehouses are like the farm system of a sports team. The smaller clubs and venues are where an artist learns to perform, gather their fans, sell their CDs and T-Shirts and struggle to make a living.

Small stages are where small artists meet small audiences.

Eventually, small audiences turn into big ones. As I said, very few of the artists who perform in places 1,000 seats or less see a nickel royalties from the PROs. So why interfere? Why charge a small venue anything at all? Even tiny 30-40 seat living room concerts are charged hefty fees by BMI and ASCAP just to let artists pass the hat to play their own ding-dang songs.

Fact: For the venues, these fees are often too high when weighed against the income potential of the room, so they shut down or cancel their music presentations.

Here's another reality check: it is hard enough to compete with TV, Netflix and the internet. Getting people to come to small concerts is a huge job. The presenters get tired, frustrated and, in many cases, go broke.

Here's where it gets really sticky:

As the market changes, as the music business declines, BMI, ASCAP and SESAC have to struggle to feed the pig. Remember the Pig? Instead of cultivating the fertile garden of music, they start squeezing the little venues for every dime they can get.

The licensing model makes presenting music cumbersome, expensive, unprofitable and, in many cases, scary. Who on earth wants to go to jail because you let a folksinger play the banjo at a farmers market? They feel at risk, so they shut down.

> **"When I hear music, I fear no danger.**
> **I am invulnerable. I see no foe."**
> *Henry David Thoreau*

By interfering with the possibility of artists to meet their own audience, the PRO's have become foes of the very community of musicians and songwriters they are charged to help.

This leaves the artists, the very ones BMI and ASCAP are trying to help, with no place to work. No place to test new music. No place to sell their CDs. No place to earn a living. No way to meet the audience ... the ultimate underwriter of all the arts.

Musician singing at a farmers market ... you guessed it: illegal

BMI and ASCAP should change their business model

Here's our reality: Only until an artist can find their audience and draw 1000 people into a theatre can they register on the royalty richter scale.

BMI and ASCAP are using an old, antiquated business model that no longer works. As that model fails, they try harder to enforce and collect fees from venues, forcing even more clubs to shut down or stop presenting live music.

We need both the PROs and music venues to be healthy and productive. We need to change the business model they are using so everyone ... and especially the artists ... can make more money.

My PROPOSAL:

I urge everyone consider a new business model, one that will not only keep venues open but encourage *more* venues to open, *more* stages to open, *more* producers to start presenting music, giving *more* artists a place to play and find their audiences.

The current model is nothing short of ridiculous. Did you know for an artist to collect royalties one of the things required is for the venue to report the songs the artist played? You know how many venues do that? Try none. The PRO's are collecting fees for songs not even being reported, for pete's sake.

I think it's unreasonable to charge the venue for the songs an artist chooses to play, anyway.

So, I propose changing from VENUE licensing to ARTIST licensing. No more harassing small venues for fees just because they are willing to create a stage for musicians to play on.

The ARTIST PERFORMING LICENSE:

With an *Artist Performing License* all songwriters, musicians and performers are clear to perform anywhere they want. *Just show your card and jump onstage.* Done.

It's like a drivers license: I can drive on any highway in America so long as I have a valid drivers license. Same with music, I should be able to perform anywhere I want if I have a valid performing license.

If an artist plays mostly small rooms, coffeehouses or non-ticketed events like farmer's markets, they pay $55 a year for a performance license. Done.

When applying for the license, they list all their original songs plus up to seven cover tunes *(the PROs now have an accurate list of who to send royalties to)* Most artists play their own material, however if an artist plays mostly cover songs, then it's $75 a year.

The ONLINE LICENSE EXCHANGE

To get the license, the artist goes to an online exchange, kinda like getting insurance. Here BMI, ASCAP and SESAC receive the accurate song list the artist is playing and their license fee is now pro-rated among the PRO's as needed. This also gives our songwriters a fighting chance to get a check from the PRO's for their songs that are getting performed ... something that is *not* happening now.

No more VENUE LICENSE:

If a non-alcohol venue of 600 seats or less, or a farmers market, school, house concert, or benefit wants to present music ... no fee. NO FEE. Done. That's it. Artists simply need to show their current license to play and that venue is in the clear. The venue simply goes to the online exchange, register the venue and what kind of music they present and that's it.

If the venue serves beer and wine: $200 a year.

Full bar: $350.

Done.

Here's why ARTIST LICENSING works:

Where there is an audience, there is money.

End of story.

Any artist would gladly, *gladly without hesitation* pay the fee knowing that - instead of three clubs in town - there are now 25 or 30 places to play. They have increased their business 10 fold.

Because the business model works for the venue, more operators would register. More stages will open.

You want to play a stage somewhere? Show your license and *boom,* no problem. Artists will have more places to perform and find their audience. And the venue will be more

Where there's an audience, there is money.

likely to actually PAY the ding-dang artists.

And, if you do simple math, the PRO's would be rolling in cash. A revamping of the current model based on the realities of the new business environment will work in their favor. For every one venue there are 200-400 artists in that region that would stand in line ready to get their performing license.

If the PROs do this they will be encouraging and stimulating the farm system nature of small venues. They need to do this. How on earth can any artist find their audience and play bigger, better paying venues when you are part of the reason so many of the venues they need to find that audience shut down?

The "ANTI" Argument

A common objection to this idea is:
"... you really want the artists to in effect pay their own royalties?"
To which I say:
"WHAT royalties???"

Remember, most artists don't see a penny in royalties. They *want* to work. They *want* to play. They *want* to grow their audience. They *want* to sell their CDs and T-shirts. They don't want to sit around waiting 14 months for their next 22-cent royalty check. So, for the love of Pete, get the heck out of their way.

To be clear, BMI and ASCAP are *not* the reason most clubs shut down. But they are, unintentionally, part of the old system that is discouraging so many venues from letting artists meet their own audience.
We need venues.
We need BMI, SESAC and ASCAP.
We need them to do well.
We need the audience to be served.
Even more, we need artists to thrive in this harsh, two dimentional digital age. *Artist Licensing* opens up the floodgates for performers to meet their audience, increases the number of stages to perform on, in turn creates long term careers for performers and develop a genuine royalty stream for songwriters.

To be clear: Converting to artist licensing will create an explosion of clubs, coffeehouses and other stages, generating an audience big enough to employ thousands of performing artists.

So ... take *that* to the bank, peeps.

Organic SongFarmer

That's really what "folksingers" are.

A SongFarmer knows the value of the *heart* over a *chart,* that music is best used for community good and family entertainment, the front porch is the most important stage in the world, that music should be more a part of your life than your livelihood.

If you play an acoustic instrument like a banjo or cello, then, well ... you're an *organic* SongFarmer.

Finding  Home

The greatest threat of injury we face in this life comes not at the hand of our enemy, but from the hand of the one who claims they love us.

Our greatest pain comes from one who was thought to be the greatest source of comfort. The circle of love has always been an exhilarating ride that, inevitably, plunges many into the shear depths of heartbreak and hell. I admire those who have been dealt kindly in this regard ... they are the lucky ones.

Love places us at great, grave risk.

The one we love has a harsh, powerful and deadly weapon at their disposal ... the ability to simply change their mind. The loss of love is our most cruel of all pains, because it is often done at the hand of one we loved, needed and trusted the most. Don't ever take for granted that the person you have deep affection for will be there tomorrow ... the first step for total loss is often complete confidence.

And trust.

There is no shield for this. No defense. No protection. No warning. We can accomplish many things in this life except for one basic fact: we can not change anybody's mind about anything. This is something they have to do themselves.

I couldn't help but reflect back to losses and love lost. Even my own. So many have felt this emotional knife plunge deep into our souls at the hand of one we trusted and needed the most.

And, my, how the walls of an empty home can thunder in a tsunami of dark stillness at four in the morning

---

And so it was one Saturday morning, a spring day in the month of April. I was off the road this particular weekend and ventured out to support the Lexington *WoodSongs Coffeehouse.* A fine hometown singer, Rennie Neubecker and his friends organized it and hold it every second Saturday of the month, at the time in a wonderful bistro with a great stage called Natasha's.

I liked Rennie's creativity a lot, and he would hold the event as an open stage starting 11 in the morning, which attracted a tremendous amount of young kids that would jump up onstage for a chance to sing their song in front of an audience.

As usual it was a pretty full house when I arrived. There were some good friends there that morning so we settled in the back of the room so our conversation wouldn't disturb the performances.

I was there for about an hour when all of a sudden this delightful, unusual voice filled the room during a song. I look toward the stage and there was this striking woman with a guitar.

OK, let's get this part straight ... the music world is loaded with a plethora of good looking women with guitars. That wasn't the attraction, but her voice was.

I had been considering for some time adding a female vocal to my opening song on WoodSongs. I wondered if she would fit? Not wanting to be too forward or even run the risk of imposing the idea, I asked a friend who knew her to see if she would be interested. She could send me a simple email if she felt like it was a good idea.

Well, by the time a friend told a friend who told a friend who finally told Melissa, she was "booked" to sing on a live audience, international broadcast that very Monday.

And she freeked out.

The next day, I'm playing my banjo on my front porch swing, the cell phone rings and it's a friend of mine who knows Melissa.

"She's totally creeped out, dude."

"How can she be creeped out, she hasn't even met me yet," says I.

And to make a long story short, we finally met, she came on the broadcast and it was perfect.

Melissa has one of those beautifully intonated singing voices, she loves music and had started writing her own songs. She was smart, a very hard worker and had a plethora of interests that she acted on.

She was a gymnast and an ice skater.

She was an airline attendent and was working on her pilot license. She had a major weather fetish and knew all the names of the cloud formations. She was a poet, a painter, an artist, a singer, a guitar player, jewelry maker and an artistic craftsman.

And heck yes, she was pretty.

Melissa onstage during a broadcast singing with a Barber Shop Quartet

Even with all of her exceptional traits, Melissa was also a bit insecure, which was attractive. She didn't have a big ego, although she could have if she wanted.

And as we got to know each other better, she loved being with me. And that was a wonderful feeling, although I was distrustful of it. I didn't want anyone to know I was even interested in Melissa out of fear it would blow up and be over. I didn't need any public disasters at this stage.

But the more I got to know her, the more inviting it all seemed. She enjoyed helping at the cabin, working on buildings and various projects. She would get down and dirty and haul timbers, logs, bricks, anything that was needed.

Melissa had a great sense of fashion and always looked pretty, she kept herself in good shape and, although I wouldn't exactly call her diet healthy, she survived well on her hamburgers and fries.

She loved to perform and on the occasions she could be onstage with me, it was great to see the audience enamoured with her. They loved to hear her voice.

That *voice*. I told her when she spoke it was almost like hearing a cartoon. I loved it.

In many ways, we are polar opposites on several things. I like tomatoes and lettuce salads. She would rather eat dirt than get anywhere near lettuce. But she enjoys gardening, so we compromise. Musically we are also quite different. I can listen to Josh White all day, she never heard of Josh White. I can expound on Leadbelly,

Patrick Sky and the Carter Family. She has no clue.

On the other hand, she loves country music, especially the stuff heard on radio. I had no idea who Luke Bryan was until Melissa did a cell phone paraody of one of his songs that got 10,000 views on YouTube and the NBC TV affiliate came to the log cabin to do a news story on it. So, we compromise. When she is with me onstage we perform folk songs. When in the car we listen to country radio.

Ee were married at the log cabin with Judge Ray Corns officiating. In short order Melissa comes to me and says,

"You know that big music room you built as an addition to the log cabin?"

"Yes."

"It will make a nice nursery ..."

"Say what??"

Yes, a baby was on the way.

A month later, she had a doctor's appointment for a check up. I'm sitting at my desk in our studio in the middle of the apple orchard in the back meadow, she comes to the door and says,

"We need to talk ..."

"How many?" says I, for some reason sensing where that was going.

She holds up two fingers.

"Seriously?"

Back home after a concert trip eating for three on my home made lasagna, one of her favorites

Life was obviously changing fast. In many ways.

Not only is Melissa going to have two babies but my daughter Rachel also announced she was getting married.

"Well, won't this be a busy summer," says I.

And, as the cosmos would have it, Rachel's wedding date would be about one week either way of the twins arrival.

"Seriously?"

Oh, yes.

Well, Rachel got married and sure enough, a week later, momma goes into labor.

We intended on natural childbirth and we were ready for it. At the hospital I paid for a therapist to come and massage her back and legs as she went deeper into labor.

I'm sitting next to her bed checking emails on my cell phone, all of a sudden a doctor and six nurses came charging into the room. In 30 seconds they had Melissa zooming down the hall and escorting me to an operating room.

Rachel's wedding day

113

"What on earth is happening?"

The twins were trapped, one umbilical cord was wrapped around the others neck and they couldn't move. One of the babies heart rate dropped way down, the child was suffocating.

I never felt so rattled, scared in my life.

But to make a long story short about 15 minutes later little Makayla came bursting into the world with one eye open, checking everything out. She looked like Popeye.

One minute later, Caleb came ... all calm and humble.

And momma was fine.

Here's the thing: we wanted a home birth but opted for a natural birth in the hospital. If we had the home birth we originally wanted I would have been planning three funerals. We came that close to losing everyone. The doctors and nurses and entire staff of the hospital were wonderful and caring. I couldn't be more grateful.

Today, as I write this, Makayla and Caleb are forever the center of her life. She is a great mom, completely attentive and in

**Momma and her brand new twins,
hours after they were born**

charge. I learned quickly my most supportive role would be to shut up and do exactly as I'm told. Which I do. Well, mostly.

The morning ritual is consistant ... daddy makes momma's coffee, oat bread toast for the babies and Peppa Pig as they wake up.

Makayla, KayKay or *"Kayka-doodles"* as we call her, is an artist, already into books and drawing and writing. And singing.

Caleb is like daddy, into how things work and music. He loves to play his guitar and has a remarkable sense of tempo.

This is gonna be one heck of a family band.

A difficult adjustment is how to manage what I do for a living inside a log cabin with baby twins and a mommy who will rip the

foundation off the house if you dare wake those little buggers up.

Normally I would sit in the evening with a banjo in my lap, writing, rehearsing, trying to work my hands. In the mornings, I am an early riser so it is usually a cup of coffee and my guitar. Most of the songs I write begin late at night and I finish them the next morning.

All of that had to be altered in deference to the twins' schedule plus still try to make a living to support a stay-at-home mom and two infants.

Part of the solution was building a writer's cabin, an artist's dream of a man-cave in the back meadow. My vision was to make it completely from repurposed materials and suitable as a recording studio if I wanted. It was going along fine until a tree fell on it in the midst of framing the ding-dang thing.

I looked at the wreckage in sheer disbelief ... all that work crushed into splinters. Oddly enough, none of the glass windows I installed into the framing broke. Not a single pane. I took that as a sign that I should rebuild it from scratch.

"How hard could it be?" I wondered.

Pretty ding-dang hard.

But in two days it was reassembled, the site cleaned up and it looked like it never even happened. Soon enough, I had my finished man-cave banjo-palace far from the dozing twins.

My completed un-re-crushed Writer's Cabin in the back meadow. It has lot's of windows that overlook the apple orchard.

Of course as I look at these pictures I realize they will be out-dated as soon as this book is published. Kids grow so fast, they grow away even faster. Before you know it, they are driving, finishing school, moving into their own apartment, getting married. Before you know it, somebody is going to announce they are having their own baby and Melissa will become a ... a ... a ... *grandmother* :)

MichaelB, Melody & Rachel

119

Yes, the circle of love has always been an exhilarating ride that, if you stick with it, can come out just fine.

Sure it takes work, and nothing is perfect. Life is like my artist's cabin ... you start with a grand dream and good intentions and then, holy cow, something unexpected happens and it lies before you crushed and seemingly beyond repair.

But it can be repaired, it can be fixed. It can be healed. And with a little time, a little effort, a little patience it all gets put back together.

And when you're done, it's as if the bad stuff never happened.

And healing can be a great adventure if you view the world, your heart and your imperfections calmly. No matter what happens, our roads twist and turn without much help from us. If it goes up, it'll come down. If it turns right, it'll turn left. Always.

Life is like the weather ... give it a minute, it'll change.

So, a tip of the glass to all on the mend, to any who have carried the weight of someone leaving, to those who have felt the coldness of a steel blade piercing through their soul as the one you love gives up ... and walks away. Hang in there. And if the person leaving was *you*, don't just forgive yourself. Get better. Get bigger. Get stronger. Get wiser. Experience will teach you that time heals and erases, cures and improves ... every building that falls, every project that fails, every heart that breaks.

We can all rebuild.
I mean after all,
How hard can it be?

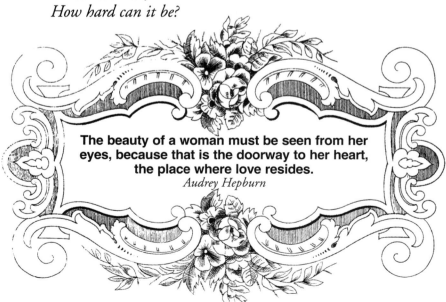

The beauty of a woman must be seen from her eyes, because that is the doorway to her heart, the place where love resides.
Audrey Hepburn

Did I mention Melissa likes to bake incredible waistline-busting home made pies?

Looking Glass

Words & Music
©Michael Johnathon/RachelAubreyMusic/BMI
Performed in the key of B
(played as if in G capo up four frets)

VERSE
It's an-oth-er fog-gy morn-ing, I strug-gle with a fog-gy mo-ment, Parts of dreams run-nin' 'round my head.

So I reach a-cross jum-bled co-vers search-ing for a morn-ing lov-er, That's the way— I want to be— with you.

CHORUS
Once up-on a time I thought I— knew I would be for-ev-er blue, Look-ing for a mag-ic mo-ment, Search-ing for my one and on-ly you. Then I found my la-dy lass— look-ing through a look-ing glass And that's the way— I want to be— with you.

It's another foggy morning
I struggle with a foggy moment
parts of dreams runnin' 'round my head

So I reach across jumbled covers
searching for a morning Lover
That's the way I want to be with you.

Once upon a time I thought I knew
I would be forever blue
        searching for a magic moment
        searching for my one and only you
Then I found my Lady Lass
        looking through a Looking Glass
        that's the way I want to be with you

Instrumental

Once upon a time I thought I knew
I would never find another you
        searching for a magic moment
        searching for my one and only you
Then I found my Lady Lass
        looking through a Looking Glass
        that's the way I want to be with you

It's another foggy morning
I struggle with a foggy moment
parts of dreams runnin' 'round my head

So I reach across jumbled covers
        searching for my morning Lover
That's the way I want to stay with you.

You can NOT pursue
the dream in your
HEART
if you are addicted to
the technology in your
HANDS

"The difference between technology and slavery is: slaves are aware that they are not free"
Nassim Nicholas Taleb

Once upon a time, folks actually talked to one another ...

Families would gather around a big table and share meals, stories and events of their day. Summer evenings were spent on front porches, living room couches by a fireplace in winter, pulling out their instruments and singing the evenings away.

Then TV and air conditioning enticed them from their front porches and imprisoned them indoors as they sit quietly in darkened rooms, barely speaking less they interrupt the Ajax commercial.

Today, the internet, smart phones, and gadgets have created the most isolated generation in human history ... all the while convincing people they have unseen "friends" in a flat-screen world.

The times have a-changed too much, perhaps. Media is in fact a brilliant, helpful tool but not if it replaces real, human, organic interaction. Media is the "paper" ... not the book.

A SongFarmer celebrates the organic musical heritage of our hometowns and the wonderful, musical world of the front porch. And we are spreading these seeds of simplicity and friendship world-wide into classrooms and for home school families. Especially schools in urban areas.

That's right ... if folks won't come out to the front porch then, ding-dang it, let's bring the front porch inside to them.

It's better to make
FRIENDS
than trying to make
FANS

Once I got to play a Clearwater concert with Pete Seeger years ago in Beacon NY. Before we went onstage a group appeared out of nowhere to meet him, to get an autograph. Pete stopped what he was doing and spoke to each person, one at a time.

When he was done and we started walking to the stage, he winked at me and said, *"it's better to make friends than have fans ..."*

It struck me as a very humble, very correct perspective. How uncomplicated, simple ... and brilliant. Beginning that day forward, I have never used that word in relation to anything I am involved in.

"Indeed, to be simple is to be great."
Ralph Waldo Emerson

**"The definition of genius is taking the complex
and making it simple."**
Albert Einstein

**"Any fool can make something complicated.
It takes a genius to make it simple."**
Woody Guthrie

**"Our life is frittered away by detail.
Simplify, simplify."**
Henry David Thoreau

**"Nature is pleased with simplicity.
And nature is no fool."**
Isaac Newton

THE AGE OF THE
"NON-PROTEST"
PROTEST SONG

"In such ugly times, the only true protest is beauty."
songwriter Phil Ochs

I made several people a tad upset recently when I suggested that we have entered a unique time in history: the Age of the Non-Protest Protest Song ... these are powerful lyric-driven songs that are *positive* in nature instead of *anti-everything*, encouraging good action, promoting community and that four letter word: "love."

Keep in mind, most of those who were upset were artists who recently released albums of protest songs that nobody was buying.

What was my point? I feel the constant roar of anger and political divide across kitchen tables, communities, the nation and the world have turned people's attention away from angry songs. Those songs don't work so well. The age of finger pointing, stomping your feet, banging your head against the wall - although important in the spirit of free speech - is for the most part ineffective.

Bob Dylan realized this way back in the mid 60s. He single handedly revived the protest song and helped it reach a mass audience. By the time his album *The Times They Are A-Changin'* came out, he found himself crowned as the King of a social movement and called "the Voice of a generation."

That's a heavy weight for a 22 year old kid from Minnesota. So, he rejected it.

Dylan had decided that this was not what he wanted to be. Within months he explained to critic Nat Hentoff: *"I don't want to be a spokesman. I just want to write from inside me. I'm not part of no movement... I just can't make it with any organization.*

Oh, yes, he gave us a literary cannon of brilliant work ... *"Blowin' in the Wind', 'A Hard Rain's A-Gonna Fall', 'Only a Pawn in Their Game', 'With God on Our Side', even 'Masters of War."* He wrote some of the best protest songs in musical history.

But he realized the work he now referred to as "finger-pointing songs" had no real value other than being musical works of art. They were indeed fine songs but accomplished little, if anything.

126

It was the beginning of the end of Protest Songs.

I'm not suggesting that you don't speak up or express yourself. Freedom of speech and freedom to express your point of view is critical. Of course, you should write, sing, march and speak up.

I'm talking about the *music,* not the intent. I'm specifically explaining why no one gives a damn. I'm talking about what works and the changes in how society communicates.

For the most part, things like Twitter, Facebook and other web-based platforms have REPLACED the purpose of protest songs. That is why they those songs are no longer effective. Good lawd ... people everywhere are arguing, lecturing, finger-pointing and complaining. It has become a harsh, loud, blustering thundercloud of digital noise that, in reality, changes nothing, changes no one's mind or point of view.

So, what replaces the protest song?

Why, the "Non-Protest" Protest Song.

Here's what a skilled writer and passionate SongFarmer can do:

Write songs that will actually work. Write songs that become noticed beyond the digital roar. Write songs that don't pound on the same bloody bruise that we see on Facebook and cable news. Folks have become weary from the anger. Write songs that make a positive point, bring community together, have a gentle approach to other poeples points of view.

These days, kindness has become a very sharp sword.

Use it. It has become even more important than ever ... the front porch should not be a war zone ... write songs that make people feel good about their homes, their front porches, their neighborhoods, their heart, their life, their community and family and that is how you can help change the world for the better. In a world of anger and forceful opinions, songs about calmness will be noticed and sung by others. And remembered ... along with you, the artist who writes it.

MOUSIE HIWAY

The Adventures of
Banjo Mouse in Appalachia

It was a fun, exciting goal ... put on hold for a while.

Before the arrival of the twins I resurrected a song and story that I've kept dormant in my mental vault for a while and decided it was time ... I want to write a series of children's books, draw the illustrations myself and publish them.

"How hard can it be?" I said to myself.

Yeah, pretty hard.

Mousie HiWay: The Adventures of Banjo Mouse in Appalachia would be the first in a series of children's books that involve music, a good story, a fun character, a valid lesson and a CD recording with the song and me reading the book as well. A musical print & audio book in one.

Alas, life, schedules and energy are not my friend at the moment so the project is on hold. *Mousie HiWay,* the first of the series, is about a banjo playing mouse that travels Appalachia, meeting other musicians and forming the *Mousie HiWay Band.* I hope to start the project again soon. If all goes well, I want hold my twins in my lap someday, reading this to them.

This feels funny because I never stop anything. Ever.

The story and accompanying CD would introduce the sound of the banjo, fiddle, mandolin, dobro and bass to young ears in a fun way. I'm not aware of another bluegrass-related children's book like this.

I like the story. It's a bluegrass lesson about bluegrass music And the rhymes.

And it's based somewhat on fact. It's true: I actually did live in Mousie, Kentucky and Blue Moon Mountain separated the little hamlet from Hindman, KY, the county seat and yes, I traveled the hollers with my banjo. Although I myself am not a mouse.

So, here is the story, read it with a 4/4 hiphop style tempo, find the phrasing. I'm including an early sketch of the Banjo Mouse character. Read it to your kids if you want. Actually, it would be great if you created your own pictures to go with the story.

Make your own children's book.

Heck, why not? *How hard can it be?*

Mousie HiWay

Words & Music
©Michael Johnathon/RachelAubreyMusic/BMI
Banjo - Performed in the key of G

Tuning: gDGBD

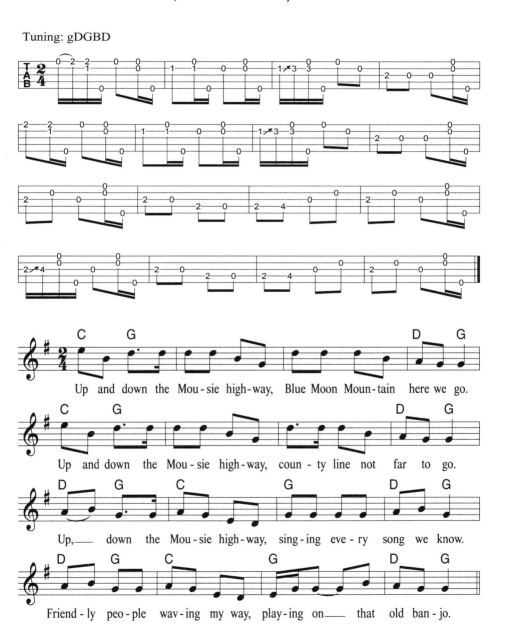

Up and down the Mou-sie high-way, Blue Moon Moun-tain here we go.

Up and down the Mou-sie high-way, coun-ty line not far to go.

Up,— down the Mou-sie high-way, sing-ing eve-ry song we know.

Friend-ly peo-ple wav-ing my way, play-ing on—— that old ban-jo.

MOUSIE HiWAY
The Adventures of Banjo Mouse in Appalachia

Characters:
Banjo Mouse, Fiddle Fox, Doggy Dobro,
Mando Moose and Little Bitty Beaver

**This is a Folk-Hip-Hop-Rap
to a 4/4 bluegrass vamp ... really.**

This is the adventures of Banjo Mouse
He didn't have a bed and he didn't have a house
But he had a lot friends where ever he'd go
'cause he knew a bunch of songs on the ol' banjo

Then one night in the Appalachian hills
He heard a lonesome sound and everything got still
In the silvery moon just sittin' on a rock
He found a new friend named Fiddle Fox

Well, he and Fiddle Fox played all night long
They played a lot of tunes, sang a lot of songs
But when the sun came up they had no place to go
till they met a new friend named Doggy Dobro

When Doggy played the 'bro he could bend those notes
He would bend them up high and bend them down low
with the fiddle and the banjo they would laugh and shout
It was a dream come true for Banjo Mouse

Now, the whole band knew that something was a-missin'
You could hear it so plain, you could hear it if you listen
So they mumbled and they grumbled till they heard the truth
When up from a holler came Mando Moose

Mando Moose had mando luvin'
He could play his mandolin, even when he was a-runnin'
He could play it so fast he had everybody shoutin'
And it echoed through the hollers of Blue Moon Mountain

Now, Banjo Mouse knew they wouldn't get far
They had a real fine band but they needed one more.
So he wondered and he pondered and he wished upon a star
And down from a hill came Kitty Guitar

She was a six-string Kitty that could pick and sing
Banjo Mouse could made the banjo ring
No one played the fiddle like Fiddle Fox could
and Doggy Dobro made the song sound good

But Banjo Mouse stopped and said "hey wait a minute..."
we have a real fine band but there's something not in it
We all want to play a real big show
but the show won't go unless we play it down low

And then though the bushes came a rumblin' sound
it shook all the trees and it rattled the ground
and down from the mountain with a smile on his face
came Little Bitty Beaver with a great big bass

Well, from Blue Moon Mountain to the hollers all around
the people all gathered for that bluegrass sound
and they sang and they cheered again and again
Everybody loves the Mousie HiWay Band!

Michael Johnathon/Rachel Aubrey Music, Inc/BMI

The Coin

"Time is the coin of your life. It is the only coin you have. Only you can determine how it will be spent."
Carl Sandburg

I was on the road with a few hours of quiet time before I had to leave for sound check. So, I'm chillaxing in the hotel room, changing my guitar strings watching a news channel.

Actually, they are not truly "news channels" anymore. They are one part story followed by ten parts of a mind-numbing panel of non-experts babbering about what think about the one part story.

So, I was half listening at best.

Then there was a feature story about an astronaut. That got my attention. You see, when I was a kid, before cartooning and music took over, I was a space freak. I loved it, even staying up till 3am to watch the space walks on TV, back when it mattered.

I discovered that you could write to the Goddard or Kennedy Space Centers, tell them you were a student interested in the space program, and they would send you a big envelope of stuff: patches, photos, posters, booklets. Amazing things. My wall was covered with posters of space launches, pictures of the moon landing. Everything.

So the story of the astronaut got my attention.

And it was a heart breaking story ...

He was a dedicated Air Force man, married with eight children. And he entered the space program and gave it everything he had. All his time. All his attention. All his dedication.

He was hardly ever home. His wife grew weary of the aloneness. Her world was her children, raising them pretty much by herself. She would spend her days on the front porch when they were in school, wishing for company, wishing for her husband.

And eventually they split, divorcing when the kids grew up.

One of the astronaut's grandsons worshipped his grandfather and wanted to follow in his footsteps, so he went into the Air Force as well, hoping to be part of the Space program someday. While flying a mission in Iraq, his plane was shot down and within months, died of his injuries.

Now, here he was: a forgotten astronaut living alone in a retirement community, his career long gone and mostly forgotten, and during the interview he looked out his window and said,

"I dedicated myself to the wrong thing."

He missed his family, he regretted what he did to his wife. And he said, *"Here I was such an important man once upon a time, such a big shot, was one of the few men who walked on the moon."*

And yet, as he walks around the grounds of the retirement community, he's just one more old man. Nobody has a clue who he was or what he did. Nobody even cares to ask.

It made me think about the passage of time. Are the things we think are so important really the priorities of what we should be devoting ourselves to? As that clock ticks, the sun rizes and the earth turns, time moves and powers through the days like a relentless bulldozer. What are we doing with these precious coins that Carl Sandburg wrote about?

Before I left for sound check, I wrote *The Coin,* it tells the story of that astronaut, his wife, his grandson ... and us.

"Time is but the stream I go a-fishing in. I drink at it; but while I drink I see the sandy bottom and detect how shallow it is. Take time by the forelock, find your eternity in each moment."

Henry David Thoreau

The Coin

Words & Music
©Michael Johnathon/RachelAubreyMusic/BMI
To match the recording put the capo on the second fret

he once flew the skies.— As a young man all the la-dies would swoon,— Now no one knows— he walked on the moon.— So he sits a-lone,— look-ing back, think-ing, I can't be-lieve— I did all that.—

There's an old man in his rocking chair,
he's got fading eyes and greying hair
Now and then he looks on high,
and recalls a time he once flew that sky
   As a young man all the ladies would swoon
   Now, no one knows he walked on the moon
So he sits alone every day,
just thinking back
Saying, "I can't believe I did all that ..."

A soldier lies in his hospital bed,
still full of shock from what the doctor said
Thru a window he sees brilliant sky
as he passes time now, and waits to die
   All he wants is to fly and walk on the moon
   Just like his grandfather did
Now he knows
he'll never be looking back
He'll never say, "I can't believe I did all that ..."

A silver lady on her front porch swing,
sits alone every day not doing anything
and as she watches the world go by,
she recalls there was a time she had a busy life
   She raised 8 children alone
   and had a grandson injured in Iraq
Now she sits alone every day
on her front porch swing
Thinkin, "I can't believe I did all that ..."

So we all have but a single chance,
to live our lives full of love and dance
to wrap our arms around a starry night,
and sail every ocean by candlelight
   Everyday is a golden coin
   spent one little moment at a time
So, live it full,
hold nothing back
So you can say, "I can't believe I did all that ..."

Yes, when it's done may we all be looking back
And say, "I can't believe I did all that ..."

The True Story of
Pamper Creek

Appalachia is a beautiful place, and, yes, I really lived in that adorable east Kentucky hamlet of Mousie for a couple years. I started my performing career there, traveling to schools, fairs, colleges and coffeehouses singing about the earth, nature and the environment.

The Appalachian people are wonderful, musical, loving and passionate. Brilliant in their common sense and ability to make due with whatever they had, working hard to manage land and mountains, raising their families, homes and traditions with pride.

Folks there really never got the support they deserved from the rest of the nation. Oh sure, plenty of welfare, but that wasn't what they wanted. They wanted work. They wanted Dignity.

They also have a great sense of humor, which helps through the realities of hardship. Between Pikeville and Prestonsburg flows the Big Sandy River. Every spring it would flood, the rains dragging all the debris from the mountainside down into the river. Folks would joke, sorta, that you can tell how high the flood water had been by where the Pampers were hanging from the tree limbs along the shore.

Now, how could I possibly not write a song about that!

Pamper Creek

Words & Music
©Michael Johnathon/RachelAubreyMusic/BMI
Here's the guitar part ... performed in the key of G - a Talking Blues

Pamper Creek lyrics:

I really love my mountain home
I love right where I am
I like the rustic beauty
of this peaceful mountain land.
But in fairness to these mountains
A story I must speak
Of a man named Solomon Cornett
and the tails of Pamper Creek

See, Solomon had a big homestead
A house and two big barns
A couple of skinny mares
And some cows out on his farm
He lived out in Pike County, KY
right off of highway 23
But his story I must tell you
And his lesson you should keep

Solomon had a reputation
For leading a swinging, carefree life
He was known to take a lover
And he was known to take a wife
One year he kept ten women
And wives, he took twelve in all
And for having these 22 woman
He had children, wall to wall

Solomon had so many woman
He had so many wives
He had so many younguns
He wished he had nine lives
He was slaving night and day
For food and bills to pay
He had 22 naggin ladies
And 48 screaming babes

One day, one of the ladies came and said
"Sol, I love you dear
But problems we have you should know about
And troubles you should hear."
Solomon struggled to his feet
And walked over to this dame
He said "Woman, I'll surely listen to you
But first tell me your name!"

She said "Sol, I looked around me and counted
twenty-two women you did take
And keeping us ladies occupied
Are the 48 youngins you helped make.
Now, all of us are lovin' woman
Sharing one man we don't mind
But scrubbing all those diapers, boy
Is a pain in our behind!"

Solomon wundered over this problem
It was a puzzlement, true, indeed
For diapers were a-plenty
As a matter of fact, diapers was all you could see.
Forty eight livin' young-uns
used ten diapers a day each each
Why it not only caused all the ladies work
but cost Sol a fortune in bleach.

So he called a meeting quick like
And said "My dear ladies, true
This problem has come to my attention.
And I sympathize with you.
So, I beg for you to listen.
For a solution I did find
To solve you of this workload caused
By forty-eight little behinds.

To help you thru this toil and work
A new invention we will buy
They're plascit, taped together little britches.
Called Pampers we will try.
Well, the ladies screamed aloud with joy
For the new invention their man had found
Just think, you could use a diaper once
And then throw it on the ground

Well, them babies went thru Pampers
Faster than a horse'll go thru hay.
48 little butt-butts went thru
500 Pampers a day
They had no place to put them
Over 3,500 in week
So, they piled em up, and loaded up the truck
And dumped them in the creek

In 1977, a flood did hit our town,
It covered over Pike County
And the counties all around
The Big Sandy River had swelled its banks
And spilled out its very side
It picked up all Solomon's pampers
And brung them along for the ride

Those waters came so mean and fast
It caused trouble for everyone
But when we saw that mountain of Pampers coming,
The whole town up and run.
Those Pampers splattered into everything
As they flooded from town to town
One fella yelled "they sure looks real bad,
But they'll fertilize the ground!

Well, that flood of '77
always comes to mind
Whenever I pass the Big Sandy
and Pampers I do find.
For, to this very day,
you can tell where the high water's been
Cause the Pampers are still hanging
From every single tree limb

Yes, the moral of this story
The moral of Pamper Creek
The lesson that old Solomon learned
Is the lesson I now speak
If you think you're such a hot lover
Then hear me out my friend
Lovin' ladies makes Pampers
And they're gonna get you in the end ...

139

FREIGHT TRAINS
Upside Down Guitars
and the
The Lost Little Girl

"There is no greater agony than hiding an untold story inside you."
Maya Angelou

It was a warm summer afternoon in Carrboro, North Carolina.

The little house on Lloyd Street was near a railroad track, and the constant rumbling of the massive trains filled the eleven year old girl with visions of leaving that mountain town and seeing the world.

The train passed by her with a rhythm, a motion, a beckoning that called to her. It made her want to jump up, run to the track and hop on that big black monster and ride it as far as it would take her.

But she was only eleven.

And from a poor home. She was the baby of the family and her four older brothers and sisters all had to work, scraping along for every dime and dollar they could muster to keep the family fed, a roof over their heads and a warm bed to sleep in.

Dreams were a luxury that a poor young black girl from a

sleepy Appalachian town could not afford to dwell on because "hopes" are like demons to a little girl with no future.

As most poor families did in 1907, they depended on simple things for entertainment, like music on the front porch. A few years ago her brother showed her some chords on his banjo. She got quite good at it and by the time she was eight she was playing several songs. Music became her comfort, singing became her escape.

And then one day, she heard someone play the guitar. Oh, my how that changed her world. What a beautiful sound. What magic.

So, she went to her parents and begged like only a little girl could beg. But there was no money. Not to be deterred, she had an idea,

"Mommy what if I go to work with you, would the nice lady give me a nickel?"

Her mom worked as a house keeper and, sure enough, the lady of the house agreed to let the child work in the home. So she saved her nickels and her dimes and every penny she could find and then one day, one amazing magical day, she was able to buy her precious guitar.

Ahhh, as fate would have it, there was a problem. You see our little child was left handed. And her new guitar was strung for right handed people.

Not to be outdone by this, our eleven year old girl took the problem and literary flipped it upside down. Yes, she decided she would learn to play the guitar upside down. Strung for a right handed player, she simply finger-picked the strings upside down and in reverse. Of course, she taught herself, as nobody quite knew how to teach anybody the guitar upside down.

And so it was on this warm, muggy southern afternoon our little black princess sat on the steps of her front porch, playing the chords on her upside down guitar as that train lumbered by.

Oh, how she wished she and her guitar could hop that train.

But hopes ... they are indeed like demons.

And the train moved on and the clock ticked and the days passed and she started to grow up. Almost. She turned fifteen and found herself married to a young man that she didn't know well and didn't like much. And before you know it our little girl gave birth to a little girl and she and her new husband, Frank, put aside most everything they loved to take care of their little family.

Including that upside down guitar.

And the days turned into months, and then years, and years turned into decades. Her daughter grew up and got married, and so she decided that would be the right time to finally get rid of Frank. They divorced and she sent him on his way.

And she never played that old upside down guitar again.

Our little girl was 60 years old now. Her child was grown and gone, and she was alone and living near Washington, DC. She had a hard time finding work, difficult as it was for a black woman in her 60's as the thunderclouds of the civil rights era loomed in 1953.

She managed to find a job in a department store. Not a good job, not a well paying one, but steady. And it was here she thought she would spend what remained of her time ... alone, in a city with few friends, living with the memories of all that she missed out on as a young girl who married too soon.

Including that odd, upside down guitar.

How often she thought of that foolish little guitar.

"Music was my refuge. I could crawl into the space between the notes and curl my back to loneliness."
Maya Angelou

Until fate beckoned again one unlikely afternoon. There, in an isle, she found a little girl lost, wandering and crying in that big, lonely department store. It was a white girl, six years old.

"Where is your momma, child?" she asked.

"I don't know!" the girl cried. So she took the girl by the hand and patiently went up and down the isles of the cavernous department store until they found the distraught momma.

Well, the momma was so grateful and overjoyed ... and

impressed with the kind, humble, caring disposition of this black woman in her sixties. As fate yet again would have it, Ruth and her husband Charles just happened to be on a search for a reliable nanny and housekeeper. Would she be interested?

My goodness, yes ... anything would be better than being alone in a big city working in this department store. She accepted the job at Ruth and Charles home to care for the lost little girl, Penny, and her brothers and sisters: Mike, Barbara and Peggy. They had an older brother, Pete, but he no longer lived at home.

And how embarrassing, after all these years, when it was time to move in, she had so few things of her own, so few belongings. It was a simple task and young Mike helped carry her few bags and a long box into the tiny room she would settle in.

One day young Mike finally asked about that long cardboard box under her bed.

What is this? he inquired.

It was that little guitar she played as a child. Of all items to keep of her past, she kept the one thing she loved and gave up, so long ago: the upside down guitar that she taught herself to play sitting on the front porch steps of her home near the railroad tracks of that sleepy Appalachian town.

An upside down guitar? Young Mike never heard of such a thing. He was taken by this new musical idea ... and the housekeeper that came with it. His excitement over her guitar surprised her.

You see, young Mike was quite the musician, his father Charles was a curater of folk songs, his mom Ruth was a singer and his sister Peggy was a folk musician and singer. And wait till she meets their older brother, Peter. Wait till he sees this upside down guitar.

Never before had this old black woman been surrounded with so much excitement over something she didn't even do anymore. She wasn't used to the fuss, but she liked it. It felt like, well ...

... family.

Finally, late one night after her work was done, she took a deep breath and pulled the box out from under her bed. She opened it up and stared at it through the lens of her big rimmed glasses, through the gaze of her aging eyes, by the soft light of her bedroom lamp.

Sitting on the side of her bed, she held it gently, almost like a timid friend that might yet run away from her. She strummed it, and to her surprise, young Mike had gotten the old upside down guitar tuned up proper before he put it away,

And for a moment, in the quiet of her room, she was that

eleven year old girl again, sitting on the front porch steps, playing her guitar to the rhythm of that nearby train, wishing she could hop that big black monster and ride it away.

And she remembered the song she wrote that same day as she dreamt of that railroad car. And her old fingers reached for the strings and her old heart reached back in her memory for the words, and she softly sang the melody, lest she dare wake any of the Seeger family up,

> *Freight train, freight train, run so fast*
> *Freight train, freight train, run so fast*
> *Please don't tell what train I'm on*
> *They won't know what route I'm going ...*

Suddenly, there is a knocking at the door. Young Mike heard her, please keep singing, he begged. Then his father, Charles came up the stairs. Yes, he said, keep singing.

> *When I'm dead and in my grave*
> *No more good times here I crave*
> *Place the stones at my head and feet*
> *And tell them all I've gone to sleep ...*

"It's just a foolish song, written by a foolish little girl," she said.

But the Seeger family wouldn't hear of it. They loved that song and, oh my, look at her fingerpick that upside down guitar. Mike decided to record some of her songs, so after school they would sit in her room and she would sing into a mic, half amused, half flattered that anyone would even care at all.

And then their older brother Pete Seeger came for a visit. *"Why, she's playing her guitar upside down,"* he said.

And word about the Seeger's housemaid got out into the music community, and everyone wanted to hear the song she wrote as an eleven year child. Before you knew it, other musicians began singing that song about the train, and they started to record the song and put it on their own albums.

Artists like Peter, Paul & Mary, Jerry Garcia, Bob Dylan, Joan Baez, Doc Watson and Taj Mahal all recorded versions of her song.

And the song become very popular.

Soon, she was asked to perform it herself in person. My goodness, who on earth would want to hear a nearly seventy year old black woman who could barely play ... and on an upside down guitar, no less?

Well, plenty. She and Mike Seeger started to perform concerts together at colleges. She began doing concerts with Mike's brother Pete Seeger, plus Mississippi John Hurt, John Lee Hooker and Muddy Waters. She performed at the Newport Folk Festival, the Smithsonian Festival of American Folklife and Carnegie Hall.

And the money and the royalties started to come in.

And finally, Elizabeth "Libba" Cotten was able to move her daughter and her family close to her again, into a fine home she bought herself and they settled into upstate New York.

She was in her 90's now. She had a heart full of love, a life full of music, and now even a Grammy Award. As she struggled to the stage to accept her prize, all she could say was,

"I only wish I had my guitar so I could play a song for you."

... that song she wrote as a wishful eleven year old girl with no place to go in the rumbling shadow of a freight train on her odd, upside down guitar.

When I die, oh bury me deep
Down at the end of old Chestnut Street
So I can hear old Number Nine
As she comes rolling by

Elizabeth "Libba" Cotten and Mike Seeger rehearsing before a concert

Knowing Your
NAME

**"The most difficult thing in life
is to know yourself."**
Thales, Greek philosopher about 600 BC

The only thing a child truly owns is their name.

It is who they are, who they belong to, who provides their home, who cares for them. And who they will become.

You don't think this is true or important?

Consider: Charles Manson's son changed his public name as a young man to flee association with his father yet still committed suicide mid-life because he could not stand who he belonged too.

Your name ... and what it represents ... matters.

And for some odd, strange, unexplainable reason, the concept of a name has been an incessant thorn in my side since I was a child and it has become a very sensitive subject for me.

As you already read, I grew up unaware that my "dad" was not my dad. My stepfather was a fine man and I grew up thinking he was my father. I was called by his last name, but when I was 12 it was revealed he was not my dad and his name wasn't *my* name. My name was different from my brother and sister.

Don't underestimate how much that hurt.

It was a defining steel wedge that bludgeoned the relationship between me and the rest of the family. I didn't belong there. I wasn't part of them. I was ... different. If I did belong, why didn't they adopt me, or make my name like theirs?

It affected every normal part of my life in a perverse way. My public reputation was my stepfather's name, but my personal records ... school, medical, legal ... were my real name. The different name. *That* name.

I didn't attend my own high school graduation when I found out they were going to read my diploma with my legal name in front of everyone. None of my friends knew about it, it was a secret. I was so rattled I ended up bailing on attending at the very last minute.

A couple years later I got married. During the wedding I was married publicly with my stepfather's name. But then afterward we all had to go into a closet so the minister could marry us again using my legal name so he could honestly sign the marriage license.

I felt rediculous and started out my married life mortified, confused, with no council from a father figure on what to do. I was known publically as one name. Yet my drivers license, wedding certificate, insurance card and everything else was another name.

"*Who the heck am I,*" was my internal mantra every day.

Noted psychologist Dr. Sigmund Freud observed deep, severe damage that dismissing someone's name does to the individual. It dismantles their self worth. I felt that way as a teenager. So, as a foolish confused young man, I fled. I revolted, rebelled and hired a lawyer with what few pennies I had and legally scoured every document that involved me and fixed my name.

And it made me feel completely isolated, it validated the fear that I was alone. Until sweet Melody was born.

Melody Larkin Johnathon. I love her, I loved her name, it was like poetry. It was like a song lyric every time I spoke it.

But an untrained, unprepared, unwise kid like me isn't good marriage material and of course, the marriage hit a brick wall.

And then it happened.

When Melody was 14 my family began encouraging her to change her name to theirs. What????!!!! Everybody started calling her by their last name, not her father's. And those disruptive seeds crept into Melody and became part of her life, it altered her view of herself ... not only confusing her selfimage but emotionally separated her from a dad who loved her dearly.

I got a legal notice that the effort to change my daughter's name was in play and I wrote a long letter to the judge pleading not to do this. I wasn't even told of the court date and before I knew it ...

... my daughter's name was no longer mine.

We were now officially different. Just like when I was a kid. Dammit. How can anybody, any adult, encourage a child to change their last name away from her dad? I went through this as a kid, they saw how if affected me and yet here it goes again. I remember hearing the news, hanging up the phone and staring at the wall for hours. I couldn't move, I couldn't respond. I couldn't think.

I wanted to talk to my dad.

Hell, I wanted to cry on his shoulder, I was so upset.

I missed the man I assumed in my heart could fix everything, even though I had no clue who he was or if he would even want to.

And the clock ticked and the days passed and months turned into years and Melody and I drifted farther apart even though I fought like hell to stay present with her. I love her dearly and am so proud of her.

But our relationship missed the one thing most of you take for granted ... we didn't have the same name. It made the presense of my father even more important, it drove the wedge between me and my step family even deeper. It made my need to be close to Melody even more powerful.

A few years later I remarried and sweet Rachel was born.
Rachel Aubrey Johnathon.

Now, *there's* a name. Another beautiful, poetic, lyrical name. And she wears it so well. Her middle name was taken from David Gate's moving song, one of my favorite ballads ever. I remember as a kid sitting in my parents car spellbound everytime that song came on the radio. Now my precious daughter is named after a memory so moving. And I took such pride in her and everything she meant.

One day her brother was born and yes, it was so deemed by the stars and heavens and angels above, he would be named after my father. Not me ... my dad. There was no way on this earth MichaelB would be named after anyone else.

And then, ding-dang it, it started happening. Again.

I noticed my wife's family began calling him by his middle name. Everyone in my world was calling him by his rightful, legal first name. This is like a cruel, emotional tug of war and a little child was stuck in the middle of this stupid control battle.

Remember, the only thing a little child actually owns is their name ... and now, again, that name was being manipulated, challenged and corrupted.

It was like reliving an unbelievable nightmare. If I was a better man, a wiser man, I would have let it go. Call him what you want, just leave the poor boy alone. But the memory of multiple names when I was a kid flooded over me, the bruise from Melody changing her last name was still painful ... so I fought like hell.

I went to court not once, not twice, not three times but FOUR times to stop the effort to alter my son's identity. He was named after my father: that is a common, normal, loving thing. Who on this good earth can't understand that? Why do this to a child?

I remember visiting my family and someone looked at my son, then at me and *on purpose* called him by the other name. It felt like they took a knife, plunged it deep inside and ran it up my chest.

He has one name. It's his. It's true. It's real.

Leave it alone.

"A good name is more desirable than great riches"
Proverbs 22:1, King Solomon

So, what's my point?

Names matter. You and your identity matters. Your identity is truth, your name is truth. Your name is important. The first job God gave Adam was to name things. BB King called his guitar Lucille, and it mattered. Willie Nelson calls his guitar Trigger, and it matters. We name our songs, even legally copyright them, because it matters.

Who you are, your reputation, your image of yourself and who you belong to is wrapped up in your name. You don't realize it until it's taken from you. Misspelling your name on a letter or award may seem trivial at first, but it matters. It is wonderful to get an award, but I have 28 of them with my name misspelled. No matter how honest the intent, it is a sign of disrespect to at least not try to get the thing right.

And one of the greatest, albeit unappreciated, gifts a wife gives her husband is when she takes his name. How many of you oblivious husbands even consider what she goes through to do that? Not many, I would guess. And there could be an argument about it being a chauvinistic practice, maybe so.

But it's a unifying one. You can't be "one flesh" with two different names, no matter whose name you choose. It makes the family the same. Dad, mom and the kids are the unified. It's unspoken comfort and identifies who they are. It makes the children belong to someone in a manner that they own.

We live in a transient, unstable, hyphenated world of broken families, broken lives, broken promises and broken people that hide their identities behind the smoke of a cyber wall.

Don't screw around with a kid's name, for Pete's sake.

**"The one thing I want to leave my children
is an honorable name."**
Theodore Roosevelt

GUN

"We have flown the air like birds, swim the sea like fishes, but we can not walk the earth like brothers."
Martin Luther King, Jr

People sure do stupid things to each other.

We argue and fight, love and praise, kill and destroy, build and plant. Our very existance is a contradiction with the rest of this universe. Here we are, living on the cusp of historic greatness, the most powerful, wealthy, inventive and global generation in the history of mankind ... and we can't stop our incessant bitching.

We have at our disposal one of the most unique, instant, powerful communications tools in the history of speech, yet we limit ourselves to 140 characters. We have a worldwide system of learning, education, enlightenment, art and music ... yet the main use of the dynamic power of the internet is essentially to get laid. Second, to propagate fake news. Third, I guess, are cat videos.

Stupid.

In the midst of all of this incredible global noise, we continue to kill each other. America is the most armed nation on earth. The biggest military force in the world are US citizens. We virtually worship at the alter of guns and our cities have become war zones, we just don't like to admit it. After all, we are a superior society made up of educated, smart people. We believe in freedom ... so long as you express your freedom our way.

And if not, well ... we just might shoot you.

Heck, even I have a history with guns. My father was a war hero, a bronze star medal winner, much awarded and admired by his fellow soldiers. That means, frankly, in real life, he killed people.

He was also a hunter.

I didn't inherit any of those inclinations. Yet, I don't have a problem with anyone hunting for deer in the fall, fishing, or raising chickens for eggs and meat. It's part of the husbandry of this earth, for millenniums and generations.

I also don't have a problem with someone who feels they need a gun for possible protection. Let's be real, we live in unpredictable, strange, dangerous times.

I do have a problem, however, with *stupid*. And no matter how sincere our government folks are, you can't legislate stupid. Stupid people don't need a gun to do stupid things. Heck, you can take down a jet and three skyscrapers with just a box cutter. Laws won't prevent stupid. Stupid transcends all laws.

USA SNAPSHOTS©

Chicago like a war zone

Number of murders in Chicago compared to American war dead in Iraq and Afghanistan since 2001[1]

Chicago
7,916

Iraq
4,504

Afghanistan
2,384

1 – As of Sept. 6
NOTE Iraq/Afghanistan total: 6,888
SOURCE iCasualties.org, Chicago Tribune, BBC
MICHAEL B. SMITH AND VERONICA BRAVO, USA TODAY

The point of my song *Gun* is simple:

You can have your gun. You can placate yourself with all the justifications and arguments you want about why you need it. You can blather on all you need about your constitutional rights, your freedom, your privilage as an American.

You can have *all* of that ...
... just don't point the ding-dang thing at me.

"I hate war as only a soldier who has lived it can, only as one who has seen its brutality, its futility ... its stupidity."

Dwight D. Eisenhower

GUN

Words & Music
©Michael Johnathon/RachelAubreyMusic/BMI
Performed in the key of E

Don't — point that gun, — Don't point that gun, —

That ain't the piece — that — caus - es peace, — Don't point that

gun. 'Cos I don't be - lieve — what I see:

A hot tem - pered world aim-ing that gun right at me. —

Tell eve - ry - one: Put down that gun. —

That ain't the piece that caus - es peace, — Put down that gun. —

Don't point that gun
Don't point that gun
that aint the Piece
   that causes Peace
Don't point that gun

Don't aim at me
Don't aim at me
Finally set yourself free
Don't aim at me

I don't believe what I see
A hot tempered world aiming their gun right at me
Tell everyone put down your gun
that ain't the Piece that causes Peace
Put down that gun

I'm not your friend
I'm not your friend
I'm not your lover, I'm just your brother
But I'm not your friend

I don't believe what I see
A hot tempered world aiming their gun right at me
Tell everyone put down your gun
that ain't the Piece that causes Peace
Put down that gun

Don't point that gun
Don't point that gun
that aint the Piece that causes Peace
Don't point that gun

THOUGHTS ON
VIOLENCE
IN THE HOME, POLITICS & SOCIETY

"What has violence ever accomplished? What good does anger create?
No cause has been stilled by an assassin's bullet.
No wrong has ever been righted by riots.
A sniper is a coward, not a hero; and an uncontrolled mob is
the voice of madness, not the voice of the people."
Sen. Robert F. Kennedy

This world seems to be filled with people who feel the only way they can express themselves is through violence.

Our society has reduced the ability to communicate down to a crummy Tweet and we no longer know how to speak with each other effectively. We don't talk, we text.

Abusers don't communicate ... they launch into combat because they have no other skills in their arsenal. They can't discuss anything without exploding like an atomic thunderstorm. They can't speak about how they feel so they react in a way often learned from a parent who is the exact same way. They scream, holler, curse, swear, slap, punch, and shove their way to make their point.

You can usually identify the abuser by how harshly they speak about their victim in public. This is true in any community, business, family, even politics.

The victim on the other hand most likely speaks positively in an effort to keep the peace and in the hopes the abuser will eventually change. Victims, by nature, have a higher respect for the family arrangement, their partner, the society they are part of. Abusers will threaten to take the violence public knowing how humiliating it can be for the victim should this happen ... in effect manipulating the victim to submit to their will by this kind of threat.

This is especially true in families and I see it often in some that are close to me. I grew up with it and hated it as a youngster and I abhor watching it now. What is especially concerning is when the abuser goes well out of their way to paint the victim publicly as the cause of all of their problems to both justify themselves and set the stage for their next abusive episode ... which they know full well is coming because they cannot control their eruptions.

Victims live on eggshells walking gently so as not to disturb the unstable nature of the abuser, never knowing what small expression, what small infraction, what small imperfection will trigger the next volcanic episode.

Victims become expert at *tolerating the intolerable,* they become patient to a fault and often respond to the abuse in silence as a way to stop the quaking. Oddly this makes the abuser even worse when you think it would calm them down.

Abusers are expert at fighting battles where there is no war, they create enemies where there's only someone who loves them, they are so insecure that they cannot accept the loyalty of their partner so in a preemptive strike they crush it and kill it and destroy it until it's gone and stand in the smoking ashes of what they used to have ... feeling insanely victorious over the destruction.

Often, after each episode of abuse, the abuser treats the victim with complete disdain and fires a machine gun litany of accusations and complaints belittling and scolding and making the victim feel like they are the cause of everything wrong in the abusers life.

Our society, our world has been conditioned to except violence in all forms. You don't like your husband - you erupt. You don't like your wife - you erupt. You don't like your president or an election result - you erupt and get violent.

There is no greater weapon in the world to change things for the better than love. Unfortunately abusers are so emotionally blind they do not recognize it when it is being handed to them on a Silver Platter.

It is a sad story human beings have repeated millions of times for centuries ... the victim who finally walks away was in fact the best thing that ever happened to an abuser.

And the abuser, ever so un-humble, will never apologize, never admit that they themselves are the cause of their own problems.

Autumn Song was written because, well, I hate to get yelled at.

It's a very simple tune and the lyrics speak loudly, so I don't have too. The banjo part is quite lovely, very easy to play. Try it, and play it next time to whoever gets mad in front of you.

AUTUMN SONG

Words & Music
©Michael Johnathon/RachelAubreyMusic/BMI
Banjo: Performed in the key of C

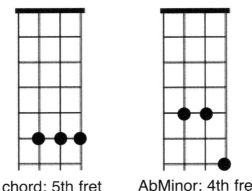

C chord; 5th fret   AbMinor; 4th fret

Tuning: gCGBD

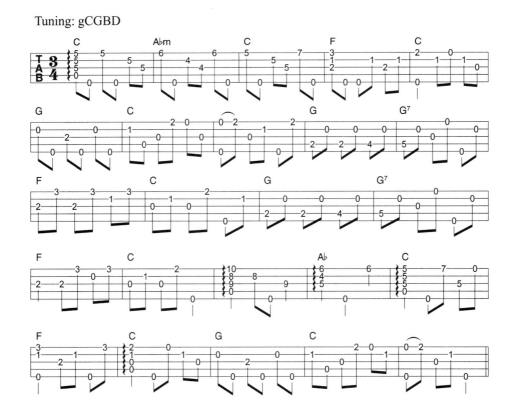

Au-tumn song, Oc - to - ber morn, is fall - ing

gent - ly my dear. Like ma - ple leaves de - part the tree,

and fall-ing gent-ly my dear. And sing to me

soft - ly; please speak to me so pa - tient - ly. Your words can

feel like au-tumn leaves, fall - ing gent-ly my dear.

Autumn song
this October morn'
  is Falling Gently my dear
Like Maple leaves
that depart the trees
  and Falling Gently my dear

So sing to me ... softly
Please Speak to me ... so patiently

Your words can feel
like Autumn leaves
  When they're falling Gently my dear

Immigrants, A River, El Weddo

THE REFRIGERATOR

"The woods are full of wardens..."
Jack Kerouac

There is a great deal of anxiety and arguing about what to do with our good neighbors to the south. Before you begin this next chapter, let me explain two important things:

Side 1: Mexico is a great nation of fabulous resources but for the last century they have been unable to provide a home that makes its own people want to stay in their own country. I'm not being critical, it's simply truth. America is a nation of "no tresspassing" signs and we happen to have a legal one along our borders. There is nothing unfair or inappropriate to expect Mexico to pay for the return of their own citizens who are here illegally.

Side 2: I lived along the Mexican border for a while and I know for a fact that most people who come across to America are not "criminals," they are hungry and poor, they are women and children, they are young men desperately looking for a job so they can send money back home to their families. They are good people with good heart and there's no reason for a "better nation," a wealthier nation, a nation of perceived morals not to treat them with care, respect, tenderness and compassion. Return them home, I suppose, is the legal thing to do ... but at least show them how to come back the right way.

Having said that, here is a chapter about my experiance living along the border in Laredo, Texas and seeing, for the first time, the human tragedy and heartbreak of families coming to America in search of a better life:

Yes ... a young me on the air along the Mexican border at KLAR-AM in Laredo, Texas. My house was a five minute walk to the Rio Grande River

After I graduated from high school in upstate New York, I moved to the Mexican border to start a radio gig in Laredo, Texas.

It happened while living in my step father's house after I finished high-school. I got a call late one night from a friend.

"Dude, you want to be a DJ?"

"Sure, dude."

That was it.

The next day I loaded up my little Toyota with 300,000 miles on it a drove non-stop to a town along the Mexican border, 44 hours straight because it had a bad starter and if I stopped the car, well ... but this is what you do when you are young, stupid and immortal.

Thus began my brief radio career at KLAR-AM and a series of jolting culture shocks that my virginal young brain had to process.

Keep in mind, I grew up along the mighty Hudson River in New York, a powerful, beautiful body of water nearly a mile wide where I lived. Now, here I am heading to the Rio Grande River, the legendary river of movies, cowboy heroes and books I read as a kid.

Wow, the mighty Rio Grande!

... turned out to be a ding-dang creek.

Literally.

All the dramatic stories I heard about Mexicans swimming across the Rio for America ... dude, you can walk across the thing.

That was my first culture shock, with more to come.

There is nothing on earth more dangerous than a nervous, nineteen year old DJ who's recently crossed cultures. And trust me, going from upstate New York to the Mexican border in south Texas is indeed crossing cultures. On the air, I had all the etiquette of a bull in a china shop. I was making mistakes left and right, mostly in a desperate attempt to "fit in." Let's face it, I was scared. My problem was that I was still so geeky that I didn't realize my faux pas until it was way too late.

Like Appalachia, south Texas along the Mexican border has its own diverse culture with a rainbow of contrasts. Where east Kentucky culture is shaped by the mountains, Laredo is in the center of a desert basin. As far as you can see, it's flat. I'm talking flatter than a folksinger's wallet. Which makes trying to drive 55 MPH on Texas hiways virtually impossible. Texans are famous for cruising 100 miles per hour or faster without blinking. This is mainly because of the tremendous distances between towns, tied together by long flat black highways so hot that they look wet as you drive over them.

The people along the border are as sweet and humble as could be. It isn't uncommon to stroll down a road in Laredo, passing small homes and shanties just to come upon a big mansion stuck in the middle of it all. Poor and rich, white and Spanish...and me. All mixed up together like a big, hot breakfast omelette.

Folks in this area also have an uncanny ability to speak two languages...at once. They call it TexMex, and the habit would keep me completely confused all the time. They would actually merge the Spanish and English languages together. I mean, a guy would be searching for his pickup in a parking lot somewhere and he would say something like: *"Donde esta my truck?"*

Being on the radio in that dual-language town was quite an experience. The station I worked for had as diverse a music playlist as I've ever experienced, before or since. We would play a popular old Perry Como hit, then a Donna Summer disco record, followed by a Henry Mancini instrumental, followed by a John Denver song, followed by a José José record from Mexico.

The funniest thing that ever happened to me in that town occurred while I was on the air late at night. And the only reason it happened at all, as I said before, was because I was a geeky kid trying too hard to fit in.

You see, ever since I had moved into town, I kept hearing one certain verbal expression over and over. A housewife would be surprised by a sudden breeze that would blow her laundry off a clothesline, and she would say *"Chinga!"* A young boy would stub his toe or bang his knee, he would say *"Chinga!"* A worker would hit his thumb with a hammer and yell, *"Chinga!"*

This term was so common, and used in such a broad, general way, I figured it must be similar to saying "gosh" or "rats" or "Oh, brother" and expressions like that.

You know, "*Gosh,* my clothes fell off the clothesline," etc.

So, I'm on the air one night, finishing up my board shift early in the morning, the record ends, and I've got 10 seconds to fill before the network news feed.

Here's what I said,

"Well, Chinga, folks...my record is ending. This is Michael Johnathon and I'll see you again tomorrow ... it's news time."

Pretty normal radio talk.

Except the phone lit up like a Christmas tree in December, the engineer spilled his coffee and the secretary shrieked in the outer office.

I was still in the broadcast booth sorting out my papers when the next DJ to go on the air came walking in shaking his head, followed by the general manager of the station. The GM carried a book titled *Learn to Speak Spanish* and handed it to me.

"Look up Chinga," he says.

So, I look up Chinga.

It means, basicially ... *"f**k you"*.

Well, I couldn't believe it.

Here I am, a nervous New York kid, and I just cussed out the south Texas listening population without even realizing it. I did the only thing I could do under the circumstances. I walked into the station the next day, hung my head high, and apologized on the air.

And, so, my education continued.

The music of the area is as colorful as the people who live there. Mariachi bands are in every restaurant and on every street corner. These are groups of strolling musicians, neighborhood groups mostly, that play traditional Mexican music with acoustic guitars, fiddles, horns and oversize acoustic bass guitar instruments. The music has a bouncy, happy feel to it. I can't help wanting to cook out every time I hear it.

That's because "cooking out" was and is a Texas passion. If I'm not mistaken, I believe it was actually the law in the state: you couldn't live there unless you knew how to grill fajitas on a mesquite wood fire. Violators were forced to eat at McDonalds.

The main industry in the area, of course, was oil. The major by-product from all that industrial rigging and drilling, aside from jobs for thousands of local folks, was the one critical item needed to create the worlds best barbecue grill:

An empty 55 gallon metal oil drum.

One of these drums, a couple of hinges, a steel grating for a grill and a blow torch are all the tools needed to build a barbecue cooker that is guaranteed to surpass any hardware store or WalMart brand in quality, durability and effectiveness. And once built, these suckers will outlast earthquakes, tornadoes, rainstorms and rust.

The trick to grilling on one of these is to do it like a Texan. Preparing to cook out in Laredo was almost a spiritual experience, and they can broil a steak fit for a God. As a matter of fact, according to Texas legend, God used to live in Texas ... until northerners moved in, of course.

The key to a good Texas grilled steak isn't in the meat.

No, no, no.

It's in the *wood* and *what you do to it before you start to cook out*. And you don't necessarily need the Texas oil drum cooker, either. Any barbecue grill with a cover will come fairly close.

You need mesquite wood chunks, mesquite wood chips, onions, the steaks (pork, ribs, fish, chicken... whatever!) and salt.

Here's what you do-

First, soak a few fist fulls of mesquite chips in a small bucket of water for about an hour. Then, clean out your grill from the previous barbecue, because a good fire needs to breath properly. Then, on the bottom of the grill build a pyramid with some dry mesquite wood chunks, NOT CHARCOAL. Compared to mesquite wood, charcoal *sucks*. This wood is a hard dense creation that burns hot and long. Fortunately, it's readily available in most parts of the country at hardware stores, etc. I'm talking about 2-3" wood chunks here, not chips. If you can't find mesquite in your area, you can substitute hickory.

Once the mesquite is lit *(this might take some time to do for the inexperienced, but worth the effort)* let the wood burn down to hot coals and spread them across the bottom of the grill.

Now, cut up some onions, skins and all, and layer the top of the hot coals with it. Just smell that hot onion steam begin to waft into the air! After that, layer the top of the onions with the soaked mesquite wood chips. Now, here comes that great smell of mesquite smoke mixing in with the onion steam. *Mmmmmm!* Once that is done, place the grill on top of the coals, and lay out the steaks and salt 'em up good.

Shut the cover, get a cold cervesa, and leave it alone for a while. The shape of the oil drum cooker allows the heat, mesquite smoke and onion steam to swirl around inside like a hot convection oven, actually cooking the steaks on both sides at once, while broiling the flavors deep into the streak. After a while, open the cover, turn the meat for another couple of minutes to quick broil the other side, and you're done.

Chinga, I get excited just thinkin' about it! Oops.

Nothing in this world is better than a mesquite grilled piece of fajitas, a hot flour tortilla, a cold Tecate' beer and a hammock about 7:30 on a summer evening!

Yeeeehhhhaaa!

The people of the region reflect this passion in their lifestyle, their food and their music. Most folks are from humble, poor backgrounds. They work hard, laugh hard and love hard.

And they cry easily.

Most importantly, they are tied by blood, brotherhood and economics to the affairs of Mexico.

Now, I'm not a politician, nor am I by nature a political person. I really don't care to be. As a folksinger, though, I'm free to observe life and comment on my musings, political or otherwise. Maybe "political" is not a good word for this. I'm really talking about a sense of humanity and welfare. If that's political, then so be it. Anyway, one night, during a late radio shift in Laredo, I found my first sense of these things stirred.

You see, after the great *Chinga* episode, I was banished to remain on the late night airwaves, otherwise known as the graveyard shift. I guess the "powers that be" decided that, if I stumbled onto any new curse words while on the air, it was better to risk offending the small, rather obnoxious late night listeners than the more proper daytime listenership, made up of many business owners who the station sold air time to.

Folks in south Texas are very forgiving, however, especially to outsiders who admit they're an idiot... like I did. So, they gave me a nickname, *"El Weddo,"* which means The Blondie, or, more literally, The Honky.

During a newscast one night, I sat dumbfounded listening to the news director as he read on-air the story of a Mexican family found dead in the trunk of a car in the middle of the south Texas desert. It was a family of four very poor people from Mexico, who crossed the border and hitched a ride into America, heading to Dallas to find work. Evidently, the car stalled and the driver left the family locked in the trunk, hiding from the border patrol, while he went to get help. The police found the car several hours later in the middle of the hot, summer afternoon, opened the trunk and discovered the steaming, lifeless bodies of a husband, the mother and two infants.

Well, I was shocked and it broke my heart.

I started to ask some questions, and learned that what happened to that family was certainly not uncommon. People who cross the border are usually poor folks who are just trying to feed their families by coming to America for work. There is a nickname for them...*wetbacks.* The United States Border Patrol's job is to prevent these people from crossing the border, and I know for a fact that these professional men and women do a good job and try to be as humane as possible. The majority of these Mexican "wetbacks" are just scared men who have only the shirt on their backs, wet or otherwise. They aren't armed, they aren't dangerous. They don't want to steal...they want to *work.*

Now, as I said, I'm not a political person, and I don't have the answers as to whether people who cross the borders into America are criminal or not. I know they are breaking the law, but I can't say they are hurting anyone. Exceptions? Of course. I know that they are taking jobs from Americans, but I don't know too many Americans who want the jobs they take.

All I knew is that my house was just a five minute walk from the Rio Grande river, and every night dozens of scared, mostly young poor people would swim across, trying to make it into the desert to catch the underground ride, usually a truck or a van, into a city somewhere to find work. Many of them left families behind in Mexico, where a dollar a day was a full time wage. They would sneak into the USA, work at an illegal sweat shop in Houston or Galveston for five dollars a day, keep three bucks to live on and mail two back to their families in Mexico.

Well, it seemed to me that the best solution was for Mexico to put its own affairs in order so poor people didn't *want* or *need* to come to America.

But I had no control over that.

It didn't help the seventeen year old Mexican boy, gone from home for the first time in his life, who roamed past my front door late at night on his way through the desert. I figured, *"You know, I can't solve the problem, but I can help that kid...".*

So, I bought an old refrigerator and put it outside my house next to the front porch.

Up the road from me was Garcia's Tortilla Factory. They made these delightfully fresh corn and flour tortillas. Every morning the scent of the tortilla factory baking away would drive me crazy 'till I was able to get to a restaurant for breakfast. I went to old man Garcia, a very pleasant round man who would sweat a lot, as I recall.

I made a deal with him. I told Mr. Garcia that I would mention his brand of tortillas on the air whenever I could if he would agree to drop off a few packages of fresh tortillas and put them into that refrigerator each day. Once I explained my idea to him he agreed.

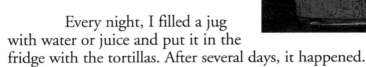

Then, I called a couple of friends of mine who worked at radio stations in Monterey and Nuevo Laredo in Mexico and told them what I was doing. They, in turn, gently and quietly let the word out.

Every night, I filled a jug with water or juice and put it in the fridge with the tortillas. After several days, it happened.

I was in bed early one morning. It was about 4am and still dark outside. I woke to the sound of muffled talking and the jingling of the refrigerator door opening. At daybreak, I got up and went outside to check the supplies.

They were all gone.

For the next several months, a steady stream of mostly frightened, poor young men would cross the Rio Grande river, search out El Weddo's refrigerator, load up on tortillas and juice, and then head out on their night time journey across the desert.

I remember one morning, opening the door of the empty refrigerator only to find a page from a Mexican bible that someone had torn out and left behind on the shelf. It was their only way to say *"Thank you."*

I picked up that torn page and just stared at it, trying to picture the man who left it behind.

Who was he?

What was his story?

I pictured him to be a good man from deep inside Mexico's interior. He crossed the river in the middle of the night, his mind desperate to remember the instructions he was told for his journey into America to find work. Did he visualize his wife in his mind as he swam the shallow river? Did he carry a photo in his pocket of the children that he'd left behind in his little Mexican town in order to sneak into the US to earn the money he needed to feed and house them? Did the image of their little faces pull him ashore once he reached the American side? Did he ache to hold them as the desert brush pricked his skin, to tuck them into bed and kiss his wife good night?

I'm sure he did.

One of the instructions he may have recalled as he swam ashore was about a place nearby where he could find some food and something cool to drink. He was told it was a safe place to come, but he probably was scared out of his mind as he arrived there because of the street light not far from my property. If he was seen, would he go to jail? He had to take the chance. He could see the refrigerator outside my door, just as he had been told, so he quietly walked onto the property.

I wonder if he thought about me as he opened the door and poured a glass of grape juice and filled his pockets with fresh flour tortillas. Did he wonder who I was? What I was like? He must have, because he was moved enough to leave a small *thank you* for me by tearing a page from his tiny Mexican bible and leaving it behind.

I don't know what happened to that man, and I don't know what happened to that old refrigerator after I moved away from Laredo to Mousie ... but me and Mr. Garcia kept that sucker full every single day until the minute I left for Kentucky.

NOTE: I hope you get my point. Law is law, I get that. But Love is love, as well. The greatest nation on earth should also have the greatest principles and morals on earth.

Fair is fair, too: if you're going to forgive an illegal resident from breaking a law, then you should also forgive a good US citizen for their traffic tickets.

It's a complicated issue, yet so easy to fix: legalize drugs to crush the cartels, educate the public to crush drug use ... and instead of building a wall that anyone can tunnel under, provide a banjo for every home in America with a front porch.

It may not solve all our problems, but we will be so busy trying to tune the darn things we won't notice as much.

'nuff said

Encouragement, Breaking Legs

and "Don't Suck"

It was one of the most exciting tours I've ever been on ... opening across the nation for the legendary Judy Collins. Not only Judy, but the great David Gates was on the tour as well, lead singer and songwriter for the group Bread.

Holy cow.

We were doing these huge outdoor ampetheaters like SPAC, Wolftrapp and others. We made our way to Chicago and the massive Ravinia Pavilion Performing Arts Center.

I would do my opening set and then run out sidestage to watch the introduction of David Gates. It was nearly the same every night. Nobody ever heard of David by name, I guess they thought he was another newbie artist like me.

But they sure knew his songs. I would rush to the audience level just as he was introduced, *"Please welcome David Gates ..."* to polite applause.

They didn't know his name but they sure as heck knew his voice and his songs. He would come to the stage with his very humble demeanor, sit in his chair, pick up his guitar and start singing ... *Baby I'm A-Want You* ...

Every concert it was the same reaction, the gasp would rocket across the audience like The Wave at a sporting event, *"It's THAT guy!!!!"*

So, this night in Chicago I expected would be the same. I'm backstage, 12,000 people are sitting across the massive lawn area waiting for Judy Collins. The stage manager, an older, kind-but-crusty fellow, is standing next to me as I await my introuction. I hear my name, he pats me on the back ... and then he said it:

Don't Suck.

Don't Suck?

As I walked onto the stage, it kinda rattled me at first. But over the course of a couple days, it kinda started to make sense. It was a form of non-violent encouragement in an effort to get someone to a good job and, well, not suck.

Actors and musicians have historically told each other to *"break a leg"* before going out the the stage. What a horrific, painful image to embrace before pouring your soul out to hundreds or thousands of people.

The actual intent behind the *"break a leg"* phrase isn't violent at all. In early ballet and opera days, it implied that you will be so brilliant you will have to take a bow during an ovation, bending your knee to accept praise. Thus, "breaking" a leg.

But these days, in this harsh and unkind political environment, I would rather do away with the violent overtones of that older saying and embrace the matter-of-fact directness of what we say at WoodSongs every night before we walk on stage:

Don't suck.

It finally came full circle when Judy Collins came on WoodSongs. She is one of the kindest, encouraginging, motivating and brilliant artists I've ever worked with. Her body of work is legendary and her voice is as elastic now as it was 40 years ago.

We were backstage, ready to go on. The theatre was full and she is standing next to me in the dark. I was thinking back of that opening night in Chicago when that crusty stage manager told me that the first time. We've been saying it on WoodSongs ever since.

Do I even dare say this to someone of Judy's stature? Oh heck, why not. She has a sense of humor.

I gently placed my hand on her shoulder and say,

"Here we go, Judy ... don't suck."

And without batting an eyelash or wasting a nano-second she responded matter-of-factly as she headed onto the stage:

"Well, isn't that the point, dear ..."

God, I do love that lady ....

I don't always speak
to Banjo players

but when I do I say
"I would like fries with that."

INDIAN DREAM

the age of the
NON-PROTEST PROTEST SONGS

Part Two

**"The way to crush a man
is to destroy his dreams."**
William S. Burrows

Peacefulness speaks very loudly these days.

Anger seems to be everywhere. It has seeped into friendships, families, communities, partnerships and, yes, politics. Fury, it seems, has become a loud, global roar. Anger destroys hope ... it destroys dreams.

So, I want to expand on my earlier chapter on Non-Protest Protest Songs as a way to complete this book.

Once upon a time, before social media engulfed out attention span and reduced our expressions and attention span down to 140 character Tweets, a songwriter would see what was happening in the world around them, write the song and the audience would listen, react, pass it on and, hopefully, sing it to others.

For all practical purposes, those days are gone.

"Oh, come on, you doofus, how can you say that ... you're a songwriter!" you might say.

Let's be truthful here: not only is the community of arists threatened by the change in the music business itself but we are hampered by how the world, our community, our audience communicates with each other.

It started with pop radio, limiting the length of a song down to three minutes. Then publications like USA Today reducing stories down to quick reads. Then came Facebook, where everyone is a writer, editor, protester, promoter, blah, blah, blah.

Then Tweeting emerged, reducing the real estate of thought down to a lousy 140 letters.

Then, finally, the death blow to protest songs:

The Meme.

A meme is an inter-netty word for those mini-billboards that make a point-at-a-glance on your Facebook or Twitter feeds. The dictionary says a meme is *"a visual idea that spreads from person to person within a culture."* Long before they became viable, the meme was described in Richard Dawkins' 1976 book *The Selfish Gene.* He felt that memes should be considered as living structures, merging visual and intelectual thought at a simple glance.

In other words: a picture is worth a thousand words. Memes were designed to replace words, compress a complicated thought in less time with less effort. They speak volumes at a simple glance.

For example, if a songwriter missed Obama, they might sit down, write what they feel and start singing the song. Others would hear it, and hopefully they would sing it or pass it on.

Now, memes have replaced the original purpose of a folksong.

These days, someone can post a meme on their social media page that says everything on their behalf and *presto,* you're done. The tsunami of social media options have replaced the power of songwriting in many ways. Protest songs are lost in the deafening roar of "anti-everything" memes, posts and Tweets. The brilliant age of Phil Ochs, Dylan, Joan Baez might be past.

Here's how serious this becomes:

If Woody Guthrie could have simply posted *"Hey, this is our land, it belongs to all of us"* in a Tweet would he have written *This Land Is Your Land?* I'm starting to doubt it. His social media posts could have superceded the music.

The power of song has been diluted because the audience no longer has the attention span to listen that deeply. Social media has trained people to *listen* and artists to *write* in brief spurts.

The "holy trinity" of music has been ruptured:

The *artist* ... the *song* ... the *audience* are no longer in sync.

The Power of LOVE

I guess my goal here is actually the end-point of this book.

Love supercedes every obstacle we face: in life, in family, in friendships, in community ... and in the music business. *Love* for your song is what the audience is looking for, not a meme or finger-pointing, head-bashing songs. *Love* puts the song, the artist and the audience in perfect harmony, perfect sync. *Love* gathers your friends and neighbors to the spirituasl front porch, the grand pulpit of every neighborhood and hometown. *Love* is power. *Love* is real.

Peacefulness speaks very loudly these days because everywhere you look folks are tense, they are angry, they are upset at the nation, the world and their communities. *Love and Peace,* and I'm not trying to get all kumbaya on you, is the powerful sword that cuts through the dark clouds covering the hearts of your audience.

Use it. The songs have become boring because memes and social media have replaced our musical voice. Anger and the brevity of the internet present a challenge for all of us ... we must write in brilliant colors to be noticed in a world saturated in beige.

Love colors everything. *Love* builds everything. *Love* is the glue that makes an artist play and write and sing. *Love* is what draws the audience to the artist. *Love* is more powerful than money. *Love* is the greatest transaction of the arts.

I wrote this book becuase I want us to believe in that again.

Be well, Create often,
Travel Safe, Sing from your
heart ... and don't suck.

Folksinger, Tree Hugger & SongFarmer
michael@woodsongs.com

Indian Dream

A NON-PROTEST PROTEST SONG

Words & Music
©Michael Johnathon/RachelAubreyMusic/BMI
Here's the guitar part ... performed in the key of Dm with Am, G, Em, A7

We do not want riches.
We want peace and love.
Red Cloud, Oglala Lakota Sioux (1822-1909)

When all the trees have been cut down,
when all the animals have been hunted,
when all the waters are polluted,
when all the air is unsafe to breathe,
only then will you discover
you cannot eat money.
Cree Prophecy

The ground on which we stand is sacred ground.
It is the dust and blood of our ancestors.
Chief Plenty Coups, Crow (1848 - 1932)

Have I done all to keep the air fresh?
Have I cared enough about the water?
Have I left the eagle to soar in freedom?
Chief Dan George, Tsleil-Waututh (1899 - 1981)

It does not require many words to speak the truth.
Chief Joseph, Nez Perce (1840-1904)

In our every deliberation, we must consider
the impact of our decisions on the next seven generations.
Iroquois Maxim (circa 1700-1800)

Treat the earth well:
We do not inherit the Earth from our Ancestors,
we borrow it from our Children.
Ancient Indian Proverb

I watch the stars
fill up the sky
Diamonds and Pearls
on a dark blanket night
Sparkeling jewels that light up the land
explaining to me the Indian Dream

In the heavenly sky
flies a sparrow so free
he lands on a branch
of a mighty oak tree
and sings out a song
that lights up the land
Singing to me the Indian Dream

So the rich man stands
in his cities of gold
jungles of steel, pipelines and roads
he struggles to save
all that's ruined our land
refusing to see
           the last Indian Dream.

Our land is more valuable than your money. It will last forever
As long as the sun shines and the waters flow,
this land will be here to give life.
Chief Crowfoot, Siksika (circa 1825-1890)

This land was made for You and Me
Woody Guthrie 1943

Album Sampler

❶ SongFarmers Blues

❷ Front Porch
(Looking Glass CD)

❸ Believe
(Woody Guthrie Opera CD)

❹ Overture/Pennsylvania Road
(Woody Guthrie Opera CD)

❺ The Dream
(The Dream CD)

❻ Looking Glass
(Looking Glass CD)

❼ Mousie HiWay
(The Dream CD)

❽ The Coin
(Looking Glass CD)

❾ Pamper Creek
(SongFarmer CD)

❿ Gun
(SongFarmer CD)

⓫ Autumn Song
(SongFarmer CD)

⓬ Indian Dream
(featuring Fred Keams on Yellowknife Navajo Flute
of the Navajo - Dine' Tribe)

All the songs on the WoodSongs III Sampler are available on
the original full-length albums except *SongFarmers Blues* and *Indian Dream*,
which are exclusive to this release ... and available at
MichaelJohnathon.com